Designing a
Fashion Collection

CLAUDIA AUSONIA PALAZIO

Claudia Palazio was born in Milan in 1968 and now lives in Rome, where she attended various institutes of art, from high school to fashion academies.

After a period of apprenticeship and internship, she began teaching fashion design in 1996.

She combines her work as a teacher with that of a fashion designer, illustrator, and theatrical costume maker.

"My dedication is to transfer the skills acquired over the years in fashion design to the new generations entering this sector".

For Hoaki Books she has published the book *Fashion Sketching: Templates, Poses and Ideas for Fashion Design*, Promopress, 2016.

Claudia Ausonia Palazio

Designing a *Fashion Collection*

16 Tutorials Using Manual and Digital Techniques

PROMOPRESS 11

By the same author:
Fashion Sketching
Templates, Poses and Ideas for Fashion Design.
The sketches used in the following pages are
taken from this book.

Hoaki Books, S.L.
Ausiàs March 128
08013 Barcelona, Spain
T. 0034 935 952 283
F. 0034 932 654 883
info@hoaki.com
www.hoaki.com

hoaki_books

Designing a Fashion Collection
16 Tutorials Using Manual and Digital Techniques

ISBN: 978-84-17412-77-7

Copyright: © 2021 Promopress, Hoaki Books, S.L.
Copyright: © 2020 Ikon Editrice srl
Original title: *Creare collezioni. 16 tutorial di tecniche manuali e digitali*

Author: Claudia Ausonia Palazio
Translation: Mariotti Translations
Editing: Martina Panarello
Layout: Fabio Troiani
Cover design: spread

D.L.: B 19801-2020
Printed in China

Contents

Introduction

In the world of fashion, the term "collection" refers to an assortment of models, composed of 40-50 complete outfits and single garments, presented by fashion houses at the beginning of the season, where 2 or 3 concepts are brought together to create a consistent, unique whole. Conversely, a Capsule Collection is a collection made up of a small number of often matching elements that represent a single concept. However, this term tends of late to be associated with collections created by top names for international low-cost chains, usually composed of a maximum of 10-12 pieces.

With this collection I wanted to show some examples of Capsule Collections, each with its own concept and realised using various illustration techniques.

A collection, to be defined as such, must contain a series of elements. First of all you have to develop a concept, represented in a moodboard of images: drawings illustrated in a comprehensible and creative way through a professional graphic presentation, notes and suggestions on the fabric and other materials you intend to use. A moodboard is like a puzzle, a collage of many images that create a single concept,

and represent the idea and convey the feelings the product wants to evoke, revealing the inspiration behind it.

We can use an A4 size or US letter piece of paper to construct our concept using images that have inspired us. These can be photos of fashion shows or a simple detail, a touch of makeup or a hairstyle, pieces of furniture, lamps, drapes, fabrics, lace, photos of landscapes or a mere ripple of water, a city skyline, ice, fog, a work of art. Every kind of content should be included on the page, a selection of found material. When connecting them, think about how the images communicate something more together than they evoke individually, and remember that even the way they are arranged can convey different feelings. If cut and arranged in an orderly and geometric way, the images give a sense of rigour. A chaotic arrangement with random cutouts will, instead, create a dynamic perception. What you need is creativity and a precise idea of what you want to convey.

Another element of fundamental importance is the choice of silhouette, as this represents the type of woman best suited to the concept. Among the many types, not just physical but above all expressive ones, we have to create, also with makeup and hairstyle, the most suitable silhouette in terms of both style and attitude. It is important that the pose should not be too dynamic so as to allow the model to be understood in the totality of its construction.

You can make collections using many techniques, but the most important thing is to use more than one at the same time so you get a wider variety of combinations, limited only by your creativity, also fundamental is your choice of drawing paper: the same technique on different paper can give very different results.

For our work to be presented in the best possible way, it has to be professionally designed. A good solution is to scan all the material and lay it out with the help of digital programs. If you want to produce a paper catalogue, you need to use a printer compatible with particular types of paper that are stiffer than the classic printer sheet. In this case, however, the sensation of touch will be lost, because if we have used a special type of paper, such as cotton or rice paper, this will not be perceived.

A collection with original designs certainly has a different appeal, that creative appeal of running your hand over the support on which the designer has worked patiently. So if you want to use the manual technique, be very careful and leave nothing to chance.

The use of card, printed images for the backdrops, colours and text: everything must be impeccable.

Hermetic descriptions, attached to each of the outfits, are appreciated only if written in handwriting that fits, and look even better on small printed labels.

Finally, a spiral binding, preferably between two thicker cards, is a good solution that makes the catalogue easy to consult. A presentation on separate cards is also fine, as long as they are placed in a rigid folder that fits in with the concept.

Now try to mix the techniques described here and give free rein to your creativity!

Claudia Ausonia Palazio

JAPAN 3D

TECHNIQUE:
collage on rough paper.
MATERIALS:
rough mixed media paper, texture cutouts from magazines, soft pastels, 6B pencil.

Draw the collection on normal white A4 sheets or US letter and trace the drawing using copy paper onto a fairly thick rough card, in this case anthracite grey in colour.

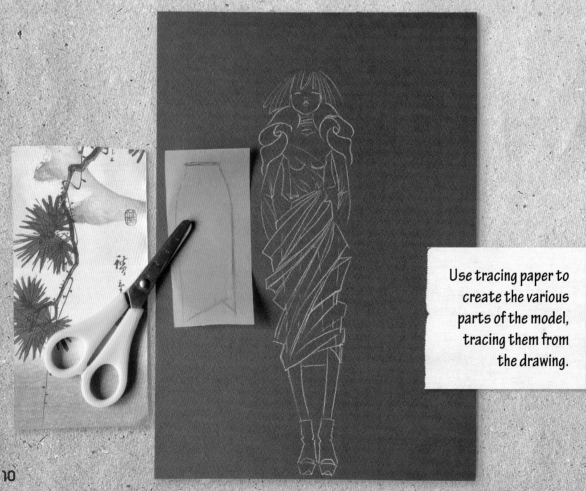

Use tracing paper to create the various parts of the model, tracing them from the drawing.

Use these small patterns to cut out parts of the garment from newspapers, magazines or collage paper. Next, paste the cutouts onto the drawing.

In this case, tracing paper was also used as a collage sheet to give a transparent effect.

11

With pencils and crayons create light and shadow to define the folds.

In this example the knitwear parts have been coloured with crayons and grease pencils.

Finish the design with soft coloured crayons for the face and hair.

Light wool gauze
for the maxi wool
neck sweater.
Jersey and
organza skirt.

Maxi wool vests.
Nature print
sweatshirt.
Silk gauze trousers.

Printed cotton
with PVC double
layer for the
bomber jacket.
Elastic tulle
trousers.

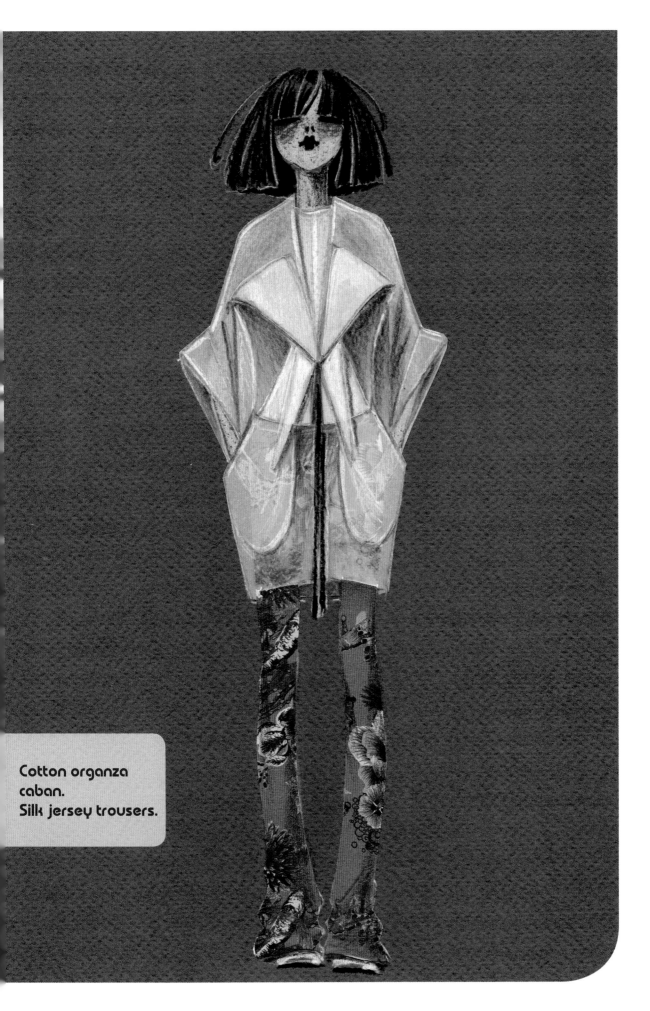

Cotton organza
caban.
Silk jersey trousers.

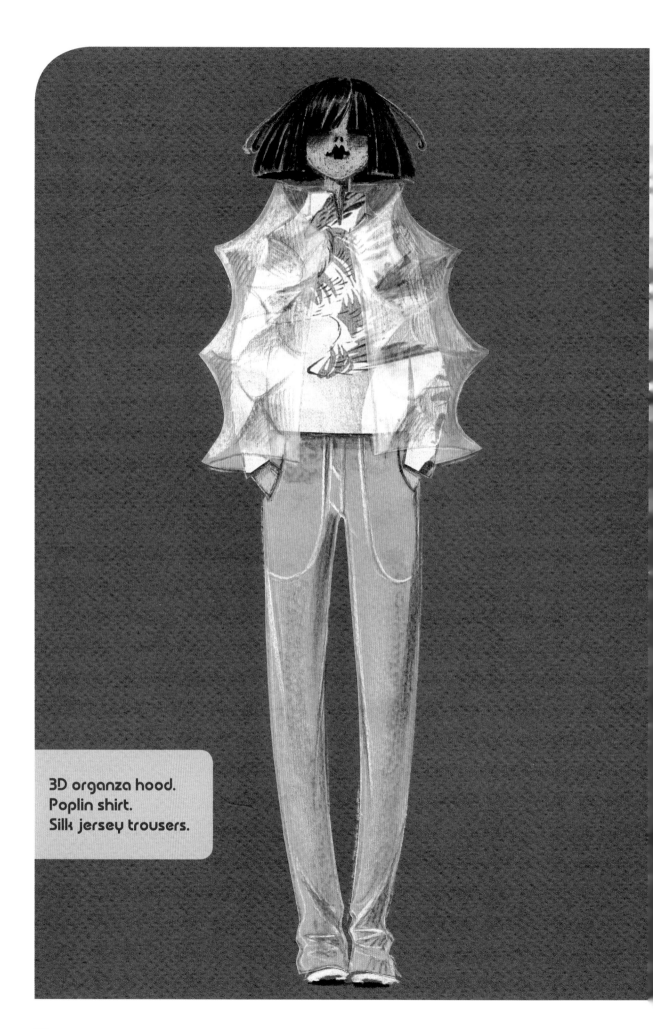

3D organza hood.
Poplin shirt.
Silk jersey trousers.

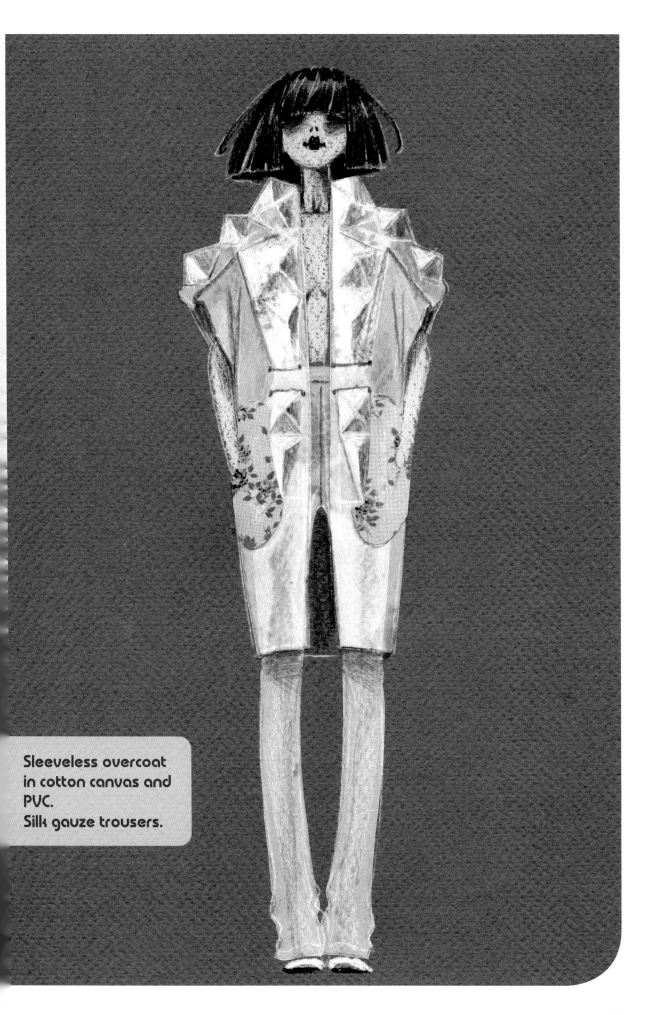

Sleeveless overcoat
in cotton canvas and
PVC.
Silk gauze trousers.

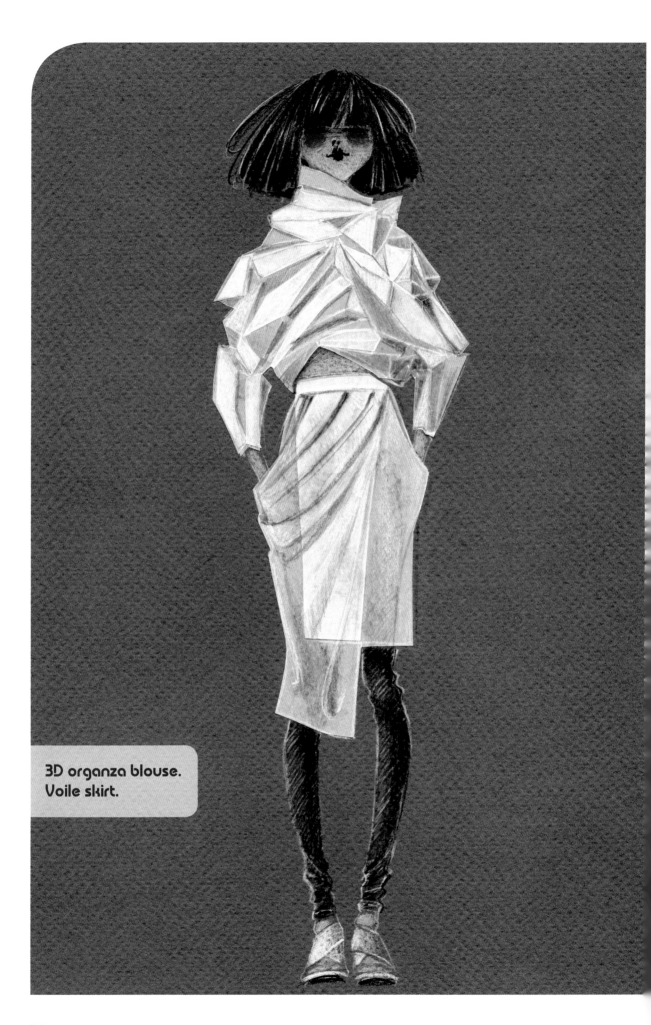

3D organza blouse.
Voile skirt.

Chiffon shirt.
3D cotton canvas
trousers.

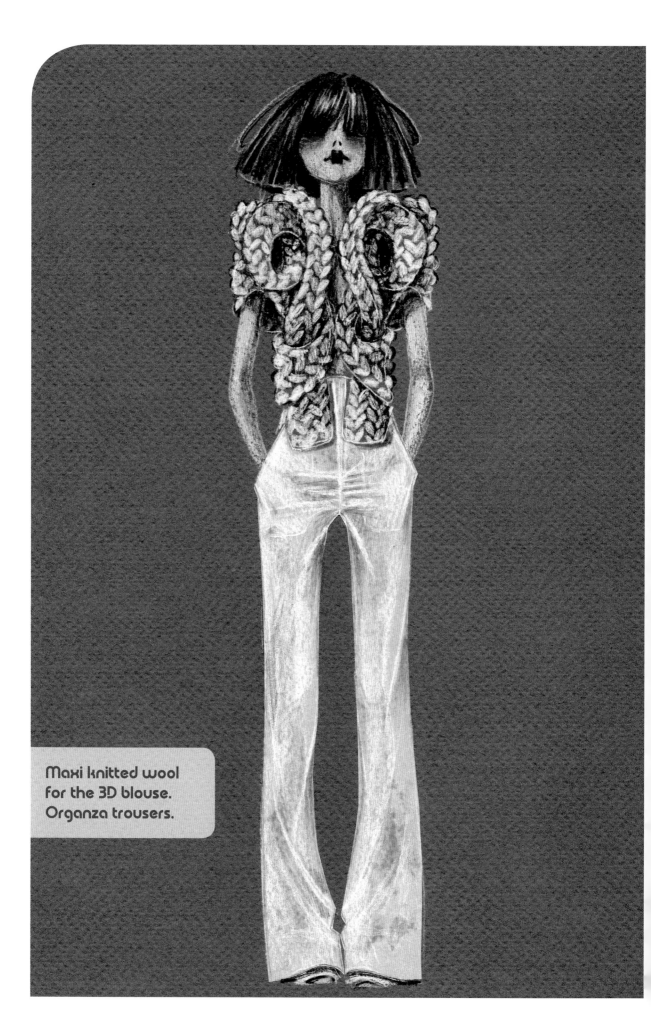

Maxi knitted wool
for the 3D blouse.
Organza trousers.

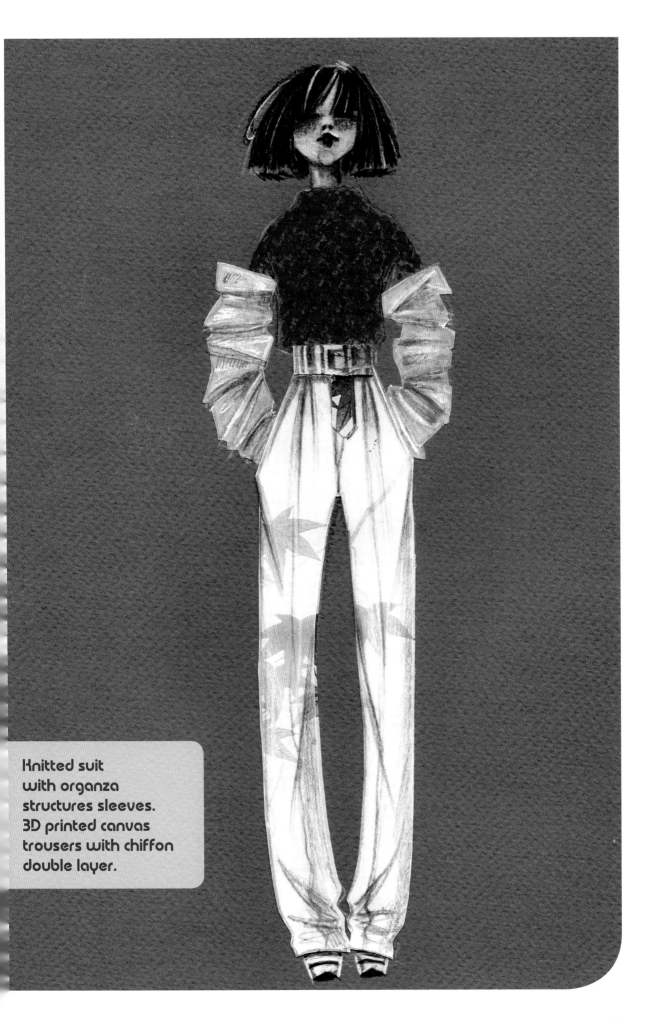

Knitted suit
with organza
structures sleeves.
3D printed canvas
trousers with chiffon
double layer.

BLACK

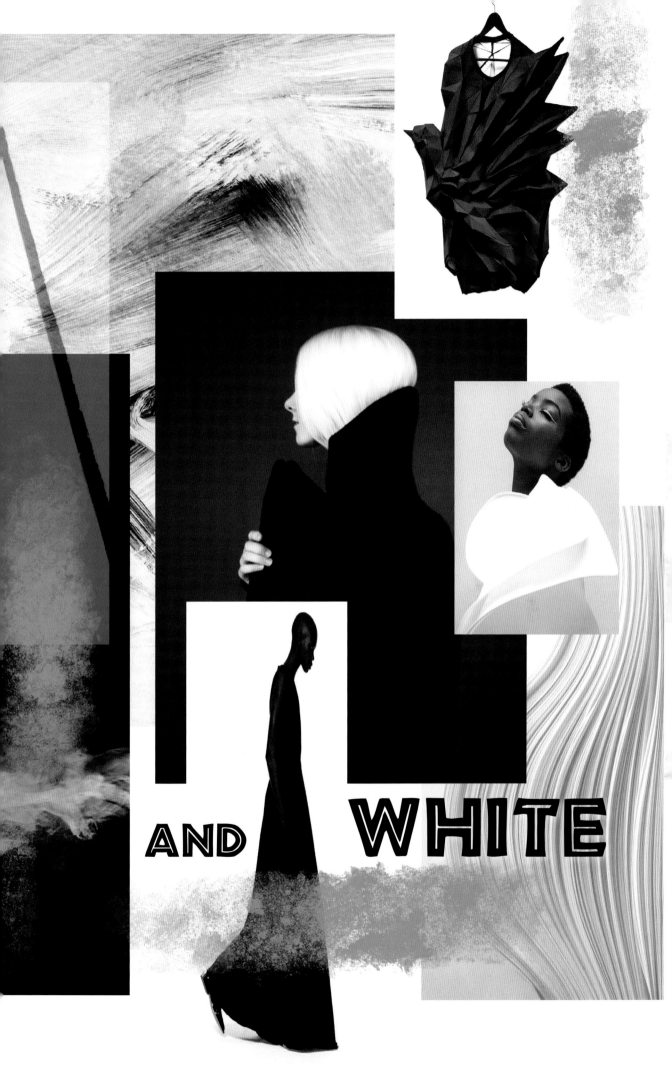

AND WHITE

TECHNIQUE: soft crayons.
MATERIALS: straw paper, soft and watercolour wax crayons, gel pens, felt-tip pen.

Design the collection on white A4 sheets of paper or US letter, then trace it with copy paper onto straw paper.

Using soft coloured crayons, start colouring the figure. The crayons need to be soft to leave bright, non-transparent strokes.

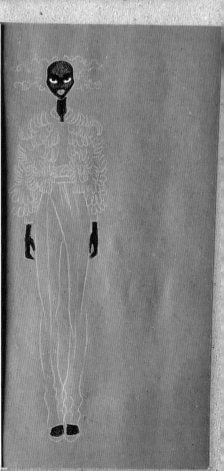

Continue colouring the figure with the crayons, highlighting certain parts with a 6B grease pencil. Finish the pleats of the bomber jacket with a touch of gel pen and the hairstyle with a wax crayon.

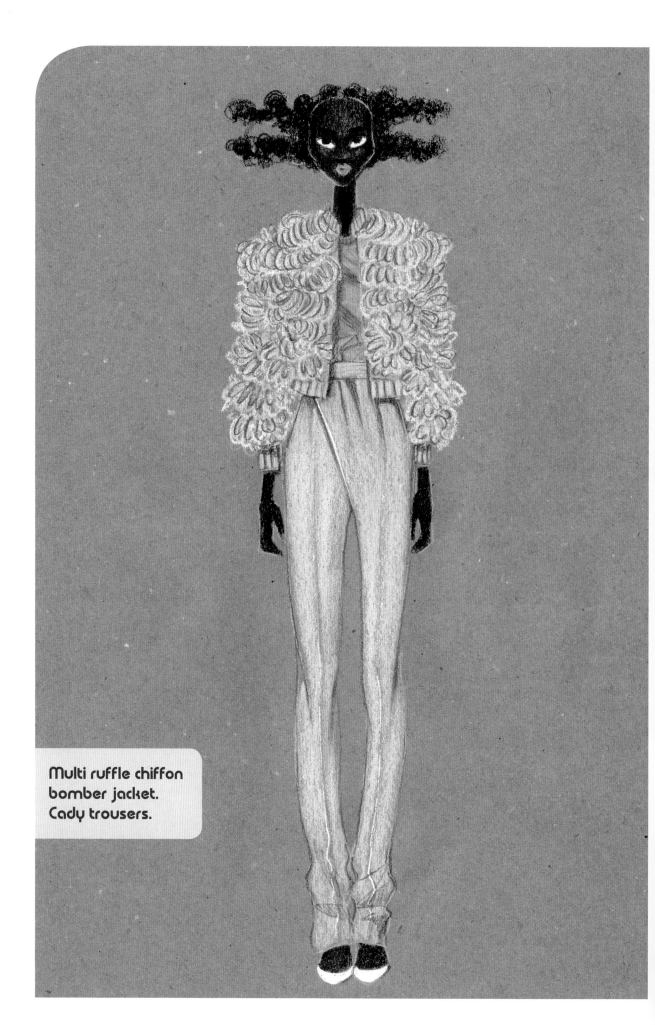

Multi ruffle chiffon
bomber jacket.
Cady trousers.

Maxi velvet
waistcoat.
Organza pleated
neck.

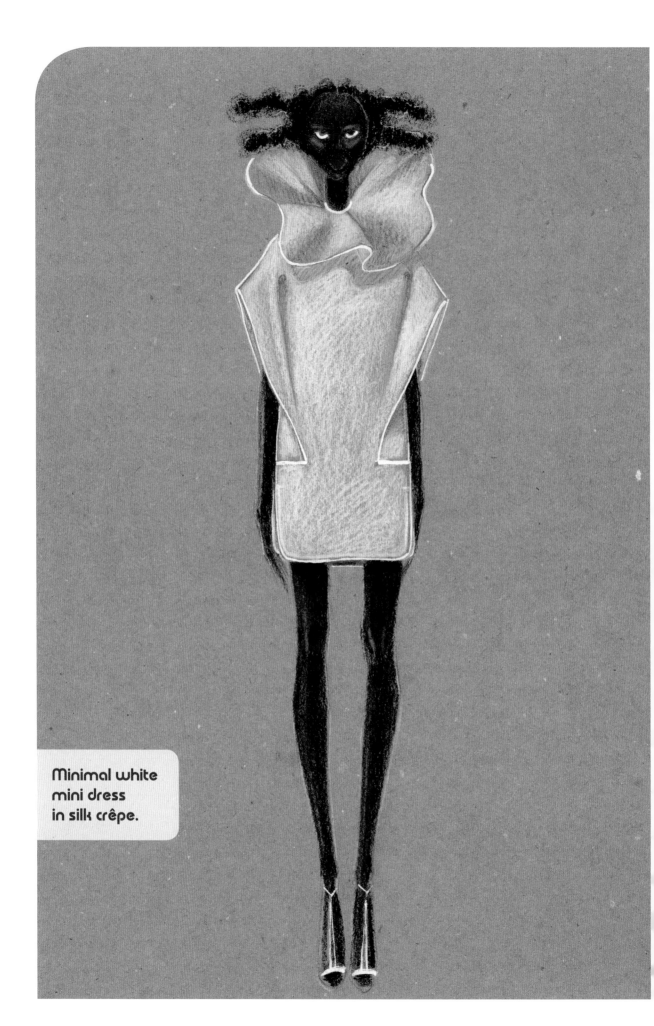

Minimal white
mini dress
in silk crêpe.

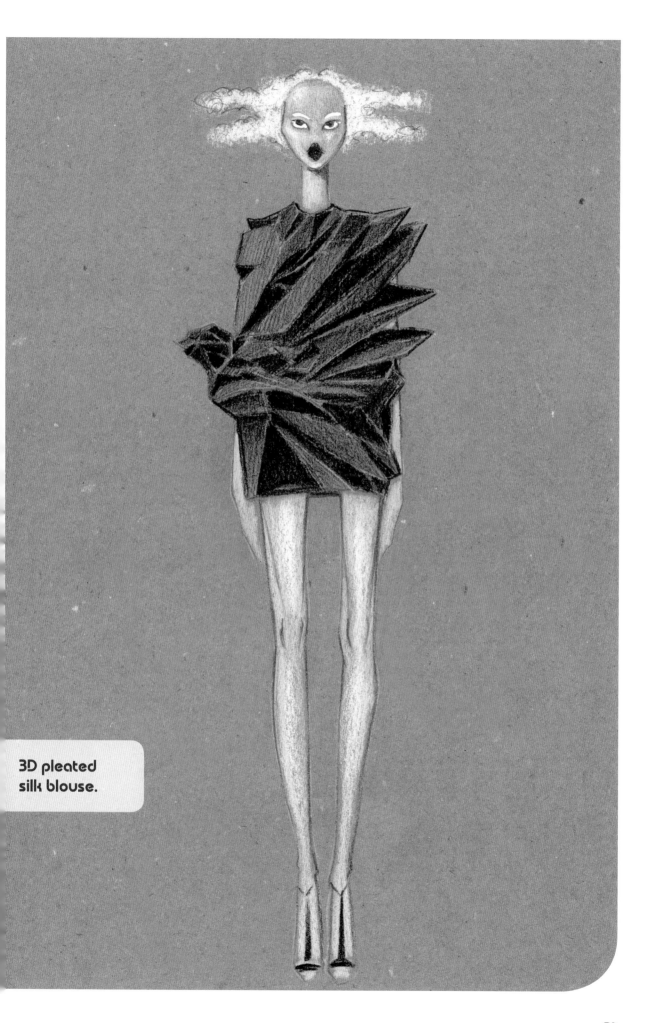

3D pleated
silk blouse.

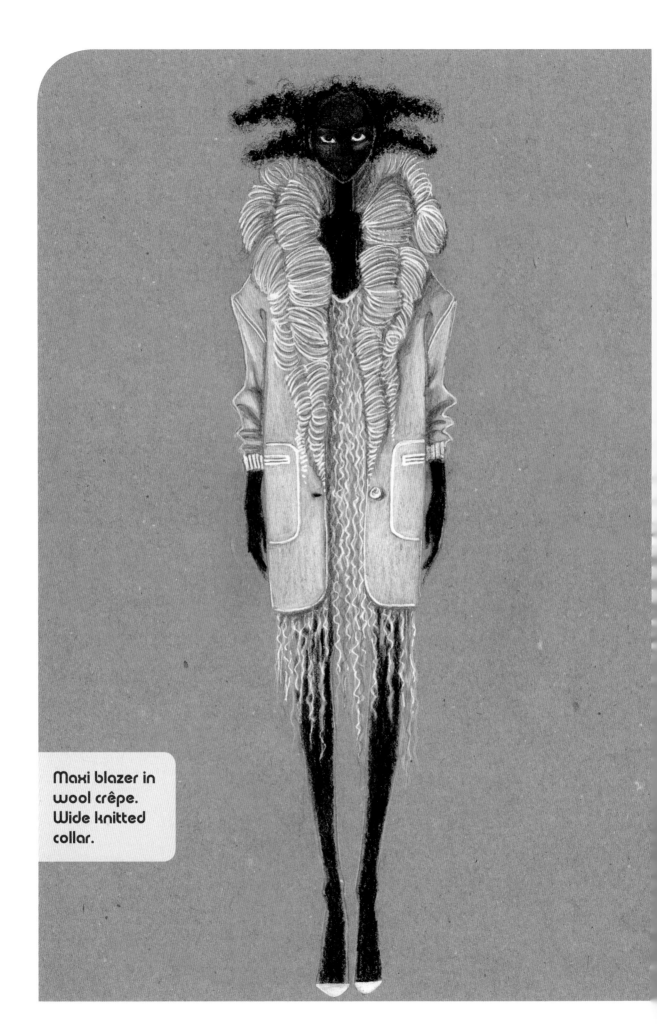

Maxi blazer in
wool crêpe.
Wide knitted
collar.

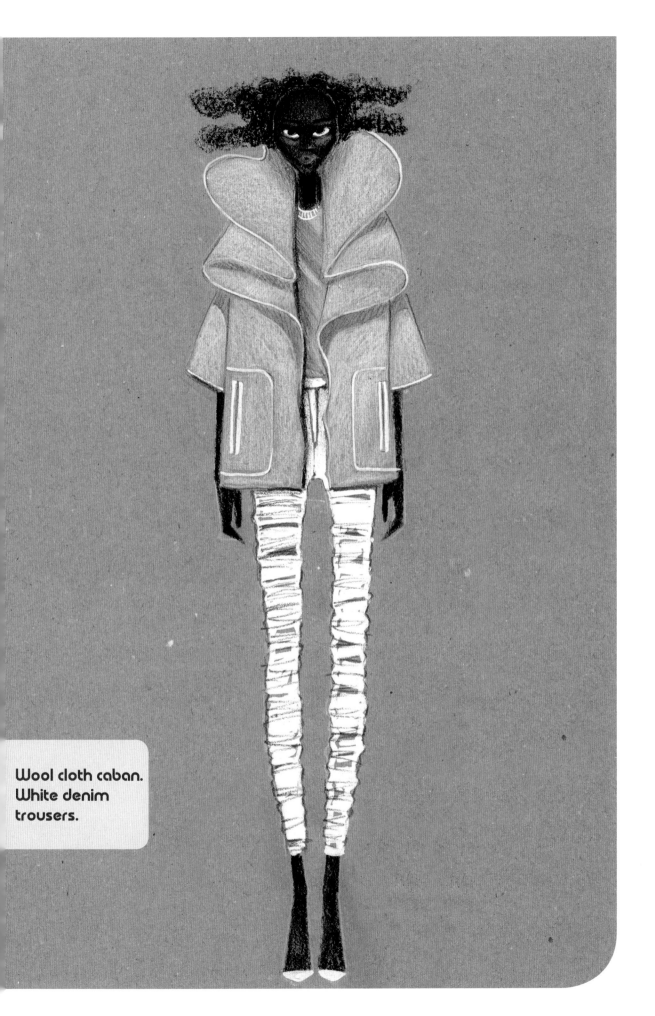

Wool cloth caban.
White denim
trousers.

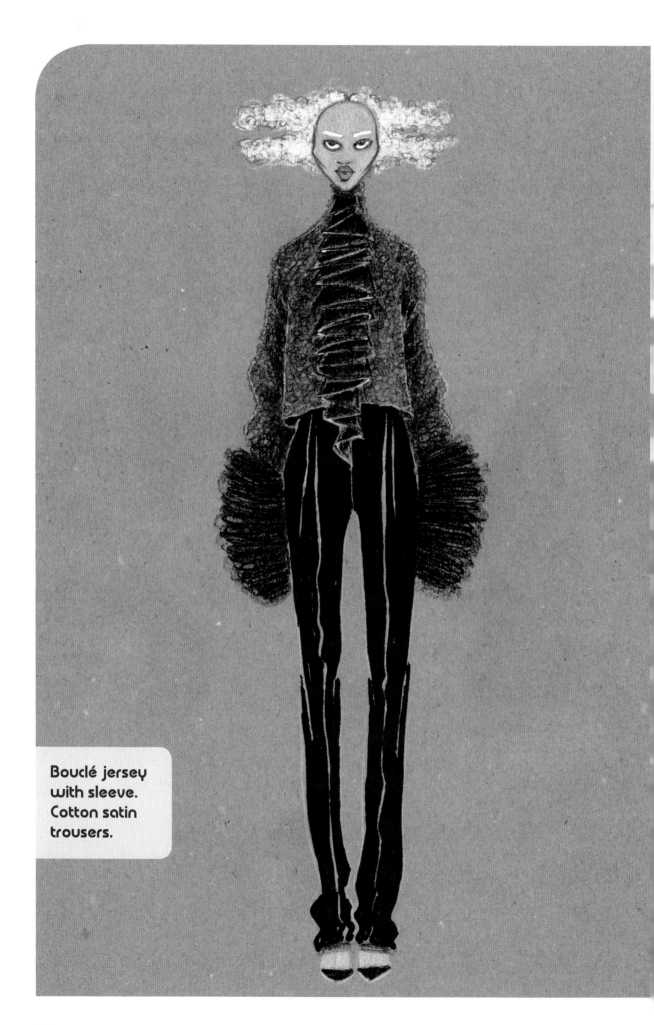

Bouclé jersey
with sleeve.
Cotton satin
trousers.

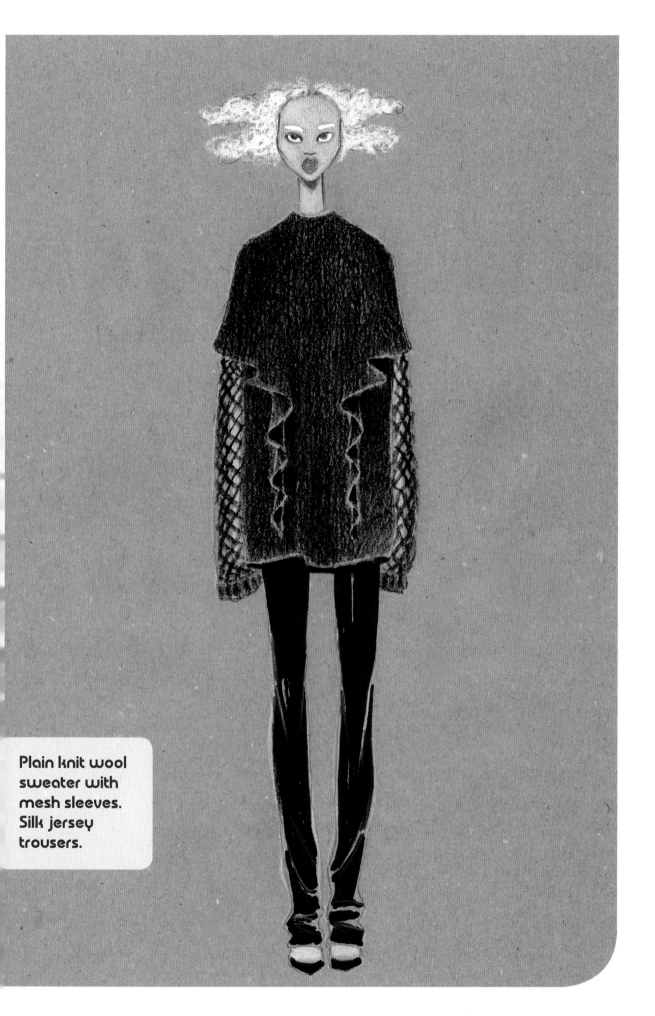

Plain knit wool
sweater with
mesh sleeves.
Silk jersey
trousers.

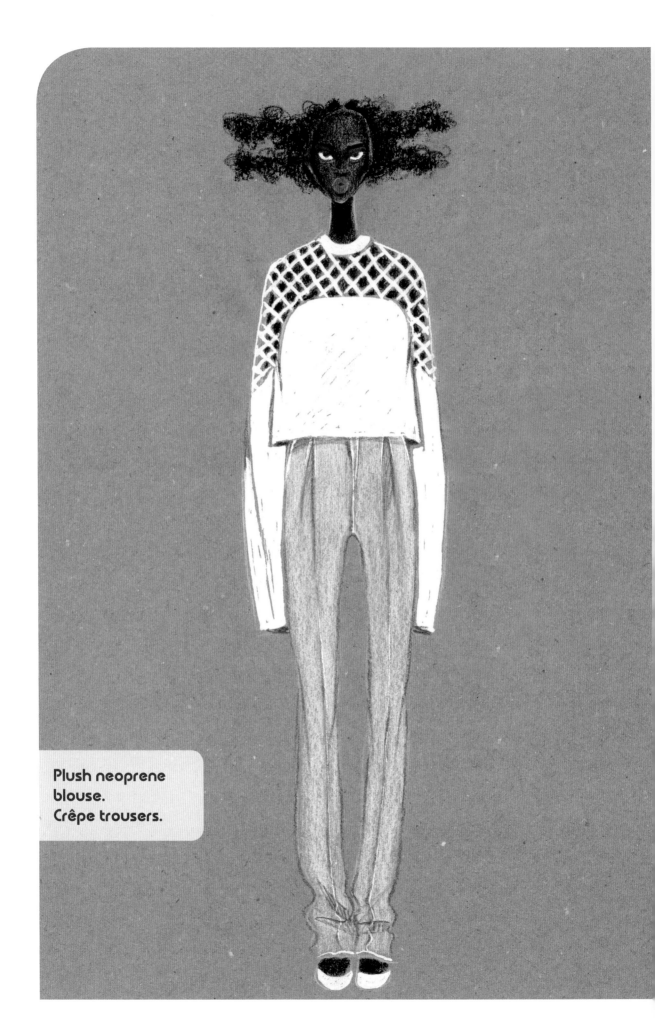

Plush neoprene
blouse.
Crêpe trousers.

Silk georgette
longuette dress.
Organza neck.

TECHNIQUE:
flat tempera.
MATERIALS:
tempera, wax
grease crayons,
6B pencil.

Start designing the
collection using regular A4
sheets or US letter as a base.

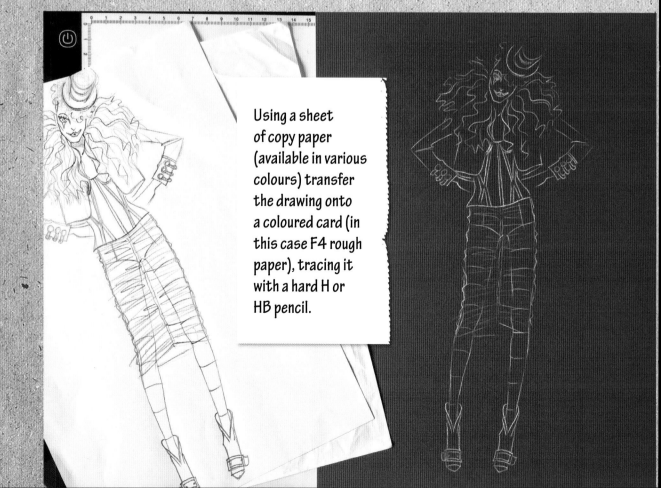

Using a sheet
of copy paper
(available in various
colours) transfer
the drawing onto
a coloured card (in
this case F4 rough
paper), tracing it
with a hard H or
HB pencil.

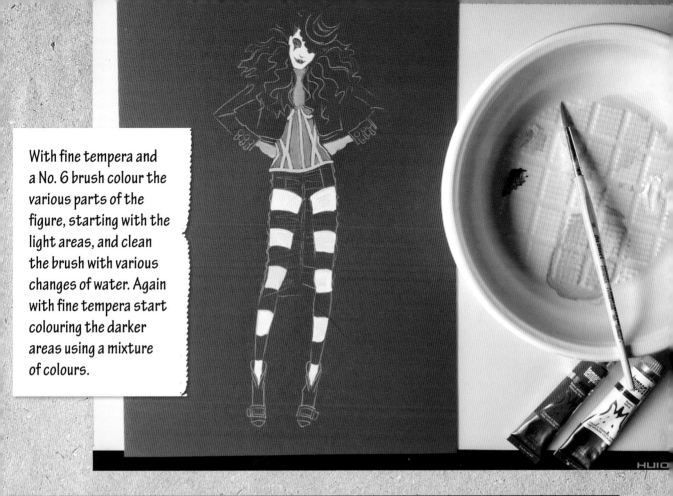

With fine tempera and a No. 6 brush colour the various parts of the figure, starting with the light areas, and clean the brush with various changes of water. Again with fine tempera start colouring the darker areas using a mixture of colours.

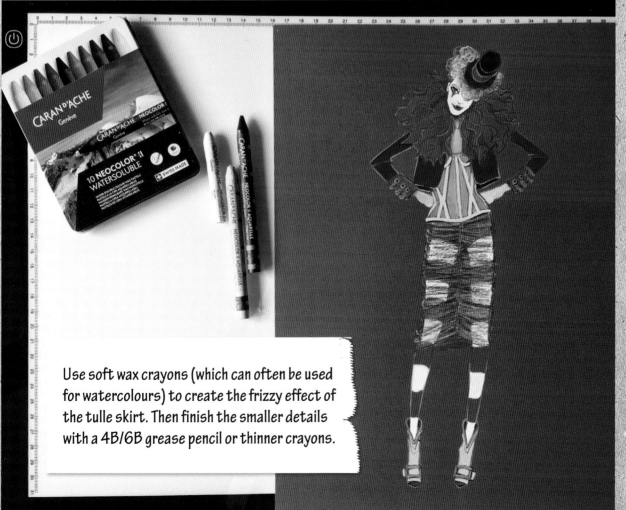

Use soft wax crayons (which can often be used for watercolours) to create the frizzy effect of the tulle skirt. Then finish the smaller details with a 4B/6B grease pencil or thinner crayons.

Crêpe and chiffon
jacket.
Tulle skirt.

Organza blouse.
Silk jersey trousers.

Passementerie
reliefs and stones
for the blazer.
Tulle jumpsuit.

Wide chiffon neck.
Jacket with frog
fastenings.
Tartan tweed
trousers.

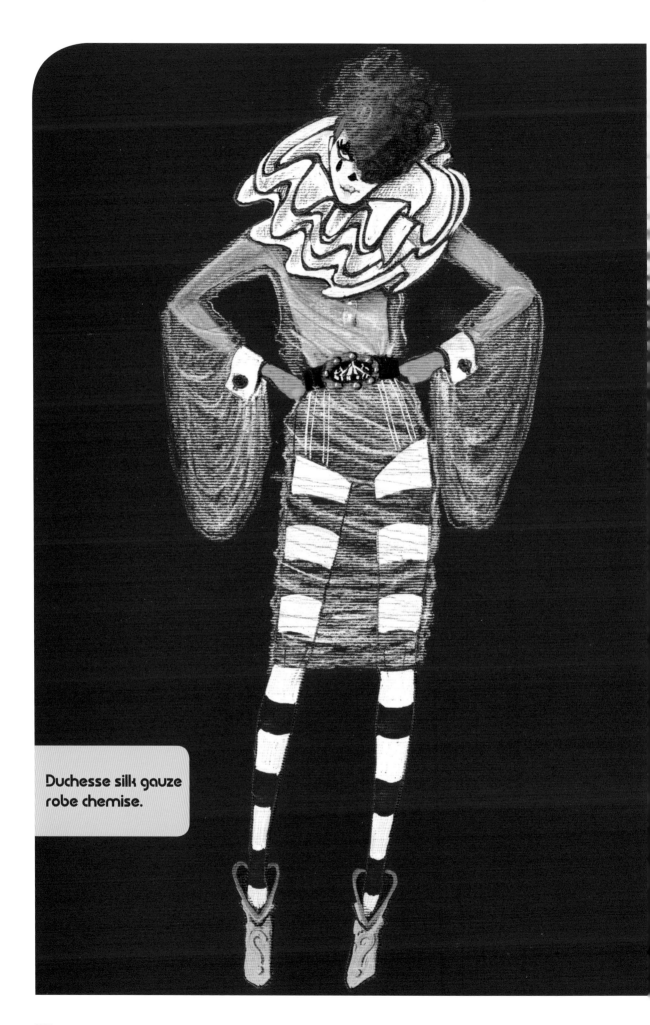

Duchesse silk gauze robe chemise.

Chiffon dress.
Tulle blouson
jacket.

Tulle dress
with dots.
Satin corset.

Skirt with studded leather basque. Jersey sweater.

Tulle dress with rubberised embossing.

Profiled mikado
jacket.
Tulle skirt.

WINTER

SEA

WINTER SEA

TECHNIQUE:
pen and ink.
MATERIALS:
F4 smooth paper, ink pen, black Indian ink, grease pencil.

Draw the collection on white A4 sheets or US letter. Transfer the drawing onto F4 smooth paper using an overhead projector and clean the drawing with a kneaded eraser.

Go over the drawing with a pen and black ink.

Use a 6B/8B grease pencil to create a slight cross-hatching in the shaded areas and blend it in with a smudge tool or with your fingers. Finish the shaded area with a kneaded eraser.

Wool cloth jacket.
Silk voile skirt.

Knitted overcoat
with faux fur edges.
Viscose cotton
sailor trousers.

Heavy wool
cloth coat.
Plain knit wool
sweater.
Stretch cotton
trousers.

Wool cloth jacket with quilted lining. Viscose jersey trousers.

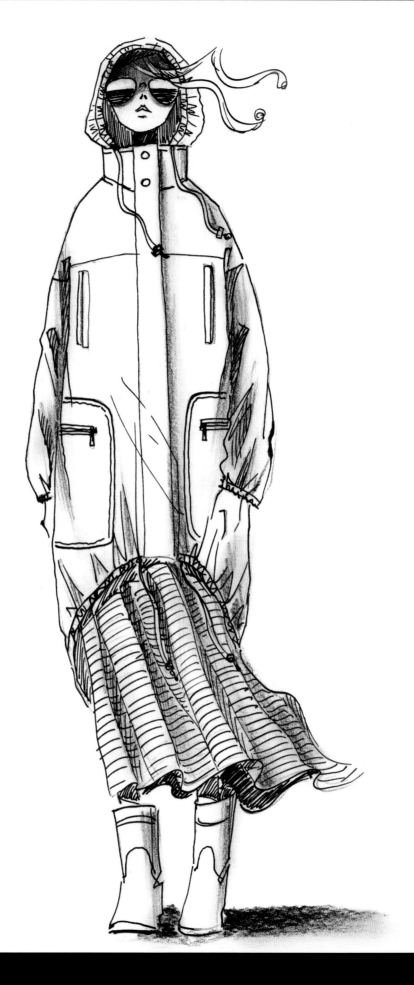

Printed canvas
raincoat.
Viscose jersey skirt.

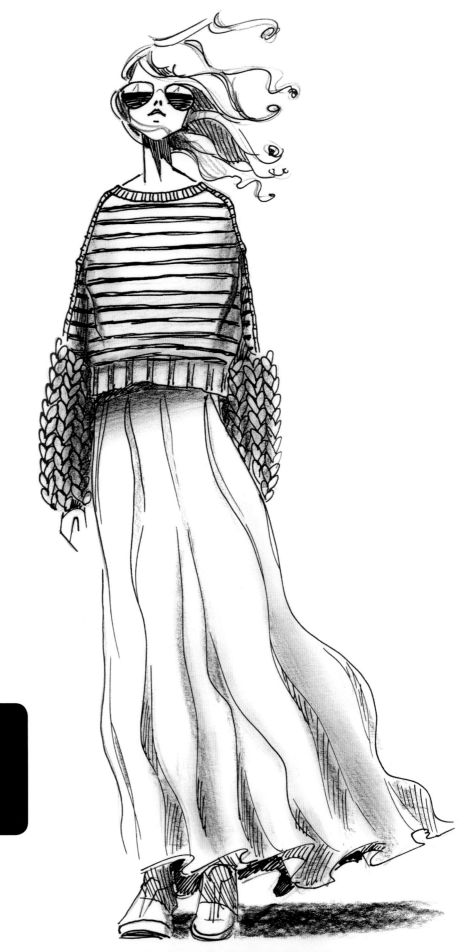

Wool sweater
with maxi
wool sleeves.
Cotton viscose
pleated skirt.

Jacquard-effect maxi pullover with faux fur inserts. Stretch leggings.

Wool cloth double-breasted coat. Viscose cotton canvas trousers.

Maxi wool inserts
on woolen
sweaters.
Voile pleated skirt.

Maxi cardigan
with ribbed knit.
Viscose cotton
pleated skirt.

TECHNIQUE:
crayon on black paper.
MATERIALS:
smooth black bristol or thicker card, grease and wax crayons, gel pen.

Transfer the drawing done on white A4 paper or US letter onto the card using white copy paper.

Colour the skin of the figure with a white crayon, very lightly touching the areas in shade and going heavier on the areas in light.

Go over the facial features with a very sharp black crayon to outline the areas in shade and define details such as eyes, nose and cheekbones.

Go over the mouth and eyebrows with a white gel pen.

Use the wax grease crayon to give structure to the hair.

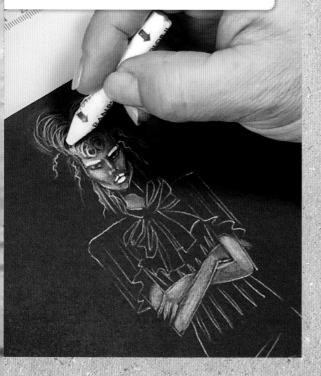

Colour the rest of the body with a white crayon.

Colour the dress with grease crayons without hiding the line of the drawing.

Define the shadows with a black crayon.

With a lighter crayon define the light points.

Use a black grease crayon to define all the areas in shadow, in this case the shadow of the figure.

Also use a black crayon to define the details of the dress, such as pleats and seams.

Smooth velvet day dress encircled with cape.

Smooth velvet day dress with ribs and faux leather fold.

Complete outfit with asymmetrical faux leather draped blouse and smooth velvet trousers.

Draped light velvet cocktail dress.

Profiled gabardine
suit.
Skirt with
asymmetric faux
leather pleats.

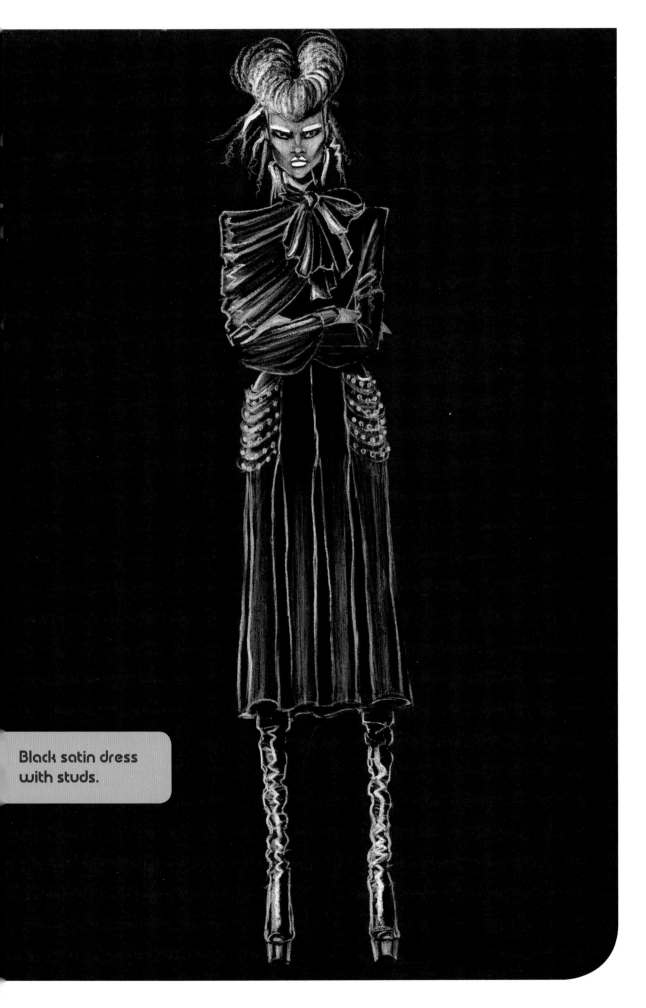

Black satin dress
with studs.

Outfit with vinyl shrugs. Light satin velvet dress with silk georgette pleats.

Wool cloth with military insignia, passementerie cord and faux leather fold.

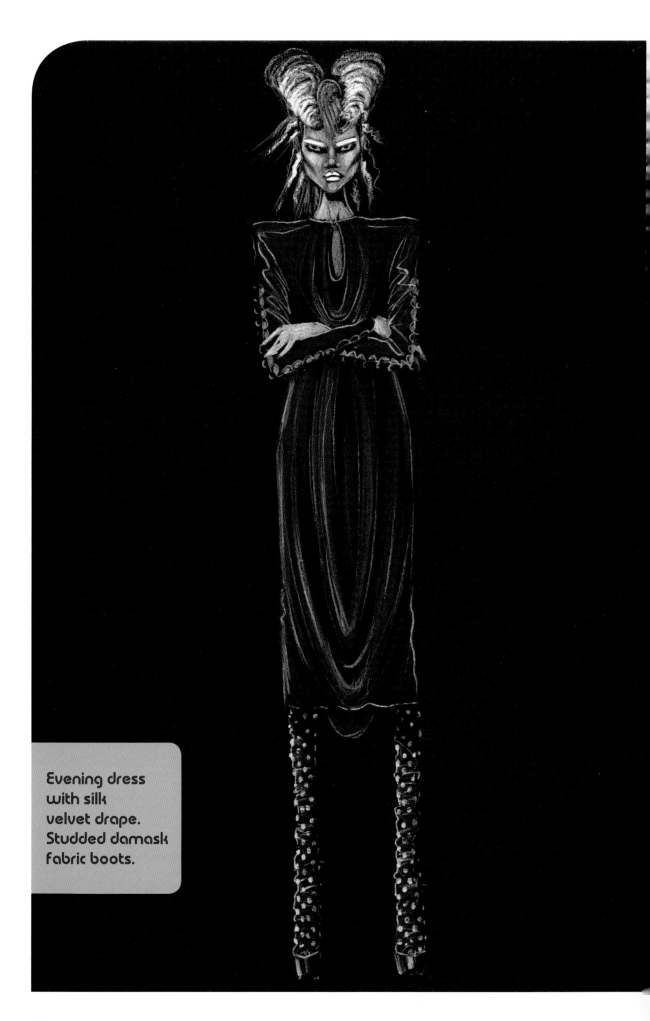

Evening dress
with silk
velvet drape.
Studded damask
fabric boots.

Elegant suit.
Velvet jacket
with cape
and gabardine
wrap skirt.

WE
SHOULD
ALL BE
FEMINISTS

Pretty
In
Pink

I ♥
80

Eighty

Jeans

EIGHTY JEANS

TECHNIQUE: gouache, mixed.
MATERIALS: F4 rough paper, watercolours or watercolour tempera, crayons, acrylic paint markers, stickers.

Transfer the drawing from the sketch on the A4 sheet or US letter onto the F4 sheet using an overhead projector, then clean it with a kneaded eraser to remove the excess graphite. Use a brush and clean water to slightly wet the part to be coloured, then go over it with a highly diluted colour.

While the paper is still wet, use a pencil eraser to create the effect of rips in the jeans.

Also use a diluted watercolour to colour the various parts of the body, like the face and hands.

To achieve chiaroscuro effects you need to change shade by diluting the colour less.

With a very sharp white crayon create a very light and dense diagonal pattern to render the weft of the denim.

Do the same thing with a black crayon in order to highlight the striation of the fabric.

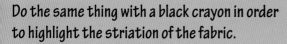

Highlight the typically faded stitching of the jeans with a white wax crayon.

Use a gold paint marker pen to colour the buttons and other metal elements.

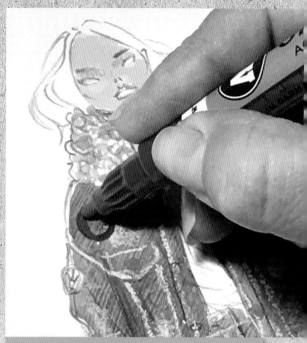

Use acrylic paint markers to colour the decorative pins and patches.

In addition to using acrylics, apply some stickers wherever you want.

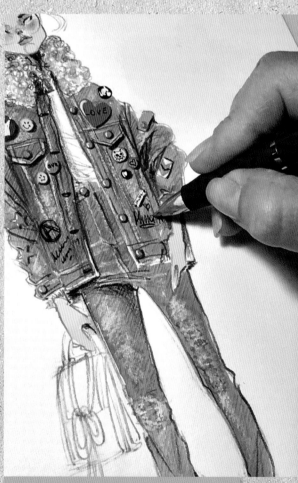

Draw any lettering you want with a ballpoint pen.

With a 10B grease pencil draw sharp shadows only on one side of the applications to create a shadow. Make sure the shadows are all on the same side. Using this trick the details applied will appear embossed.

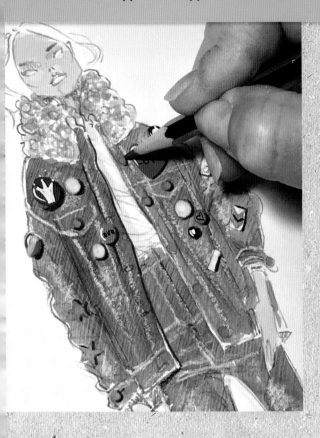

Also using a very sharp 10B pencil go over the outline of the drawing.
You can finish the drawing by creating a light make-up with coloured crayons.

Add the figure's shadow to give it depth.

Outfit with
classic 80s
denim jacket
with decorative
pins and patches,
and bouclé
wool collar.
High waist
trousers.
Suede bag.

Denim apron dress with wool trim. Coloured faux leather tolfa bag.

Outfit with short jacket with visible wool stitching and applied pins. High waist oversize trousers. Suede and faux leather bag.

Maxi bomber jacket
with a striped
denim neck and
applied pearls.
High waist trousers
and petticoat top.
Gold-coloured
suede and faux
leather bag.

Denim overcoat with large bouclé wool lapels and applied pins. Trousers with ruffle bottom. Synthetic leather bag.

Denim jacket
with straps and
applied pins.
High waist jeans
for men with a
lighter tone.
Patent leather
tolfa bag.

Denim overalls
with wool trim.
Sweatshirt with
straps and
applied pearls.
Suede shopping
bag.

Denim jumpsuit
with wool padding.
Rib knitted trousers.
Synthetic leather
tolfa bag.

Dress with
shoulder straps,
pockets and
elastic waistband.
Applied pins and
patches. Suede
and patent
leather bag.

Denim jacket with large ruffle sleeves and applied pearls. Flared trousers. Leather shoulder bag.

Accidentally

Animalier

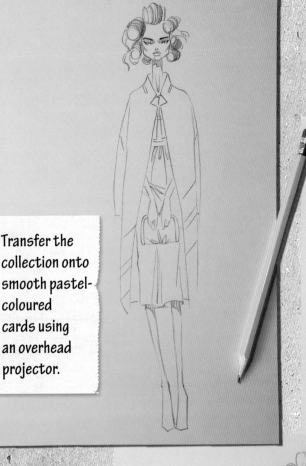

TECHNIQUE: crayons, grease pencil.
MATERIAL: smooth pastel-coloured card,
6B/10B grease pencil, grease or watercolour
crayons, paint markers.

Transfer the collection onto smooth pastel-coloured cards using an overhead projector.

Use grease crayons to colour the figure's complexion.

Also use grease crayons and a 2B pencil to complete the parts of the face creating a chiaroscuro effect.

Use a 8B/10B grease pencil to create a zebra effect or any other animal pattern. Define the glasses and curlers with paint markers.

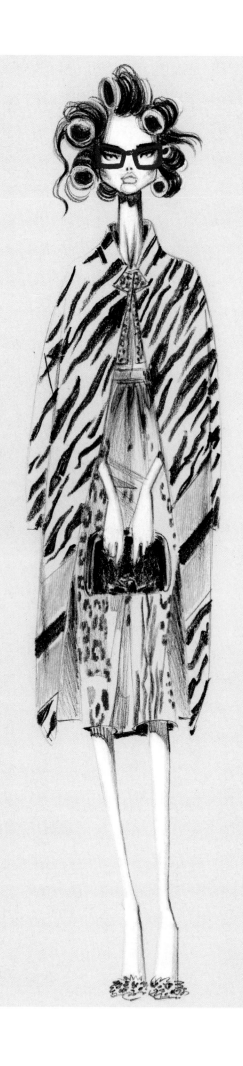

Cavallino leather
coat with
satin inserts.
Printed satin skirt.
Spotted
minicardigan.

Jacket with
printed faille
ruffled sleeves.
Satin dress.

Faux leather
jacket with
spotted short hair.
Cotton dress with
thread reliefs.

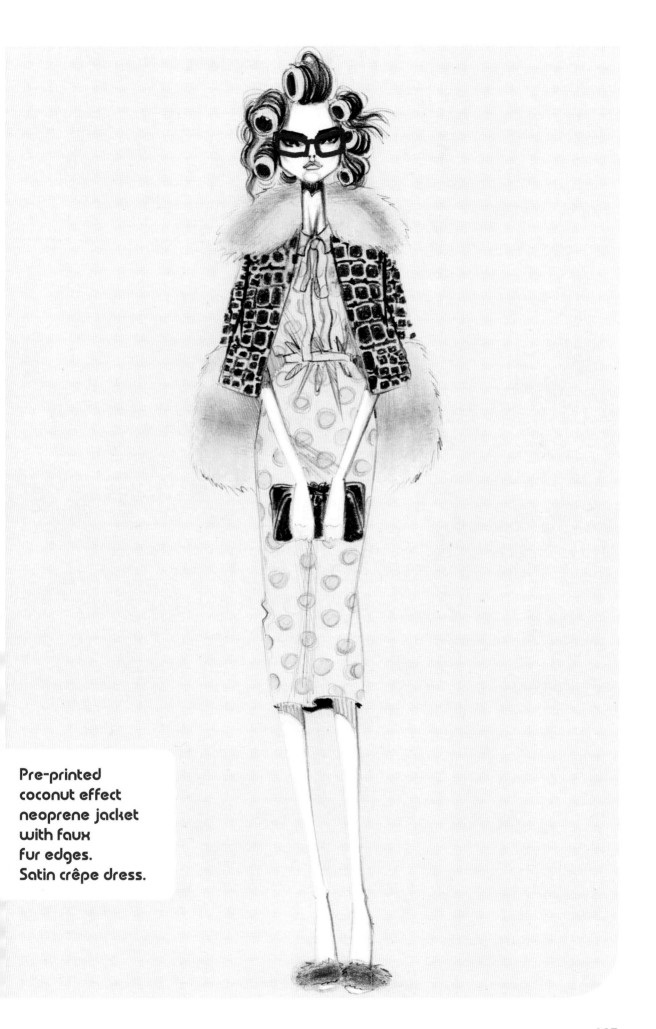

Pre-printed
coconut effect
neoprene jacket
with faux
fur edges.
Satin crêpe dress.

Cavallino leather
overcoat with taffeta
ruffles. Bustier
surrounded with lace.
Double chiffon skirt with
beaded embroidery.

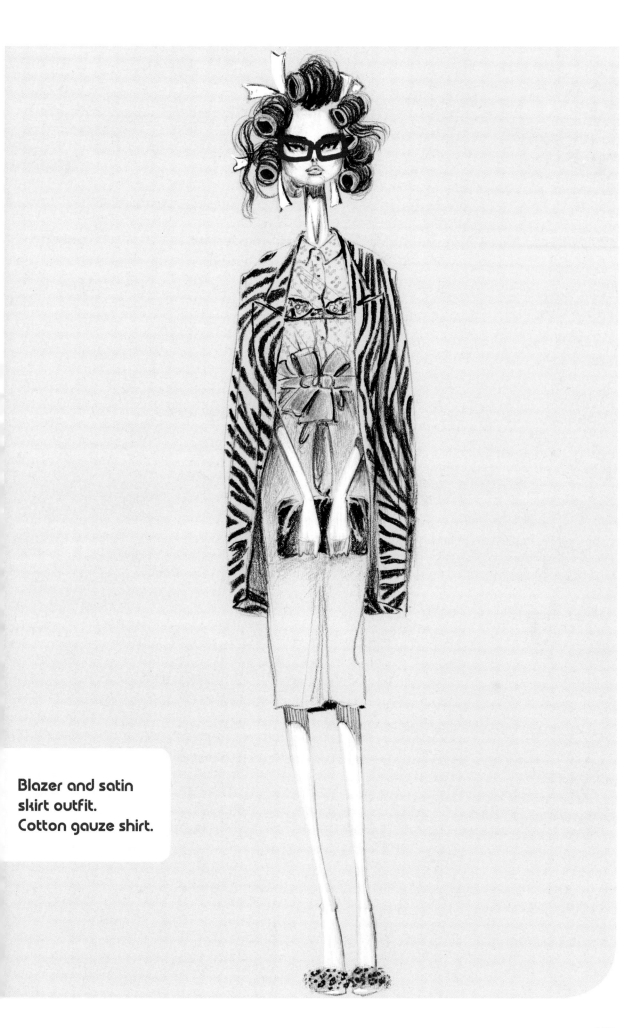

Blazer and satin
skirt outfit.
Cotton gauze shirt.

Heavy satin coat with faux fur collar. Cotton muslin dress with thread reliefs.

Cheetah effect
faux fur coat.
Georgette shirt.
Satin skirt.

Knitted blazer.
Voile shirt.
Satin skirt with
thread reliefs.

Double chiffon
bomber jacket
with quilted
lining. Gauze
sweatshirt.
Cady skirt.

Black
Style

TECHNIQUE:
flat tempera.
MATERIALS:
mixed media card
for watercolour,
tempera, 6B
grease pencil.

After drawing the
collection on white A4
sheets or US letter,
transfer it using copy
paper onto grey/beige
Canson mixed media
sheets. Use a pencil to
redraw the outline of
the figure where it is not
clearly visible.

Use the right density
of tempera to create
more solid effects on
the face, legs, and arms,
or more transparent
effects on the shirt.
Dilute the tempera
accordingly with water
to achieve the desired
results.

Finish the drawing with black tempera and add a few touches of grease pencil if necessary.

Chiffon shirt
with ribs.
Wool fabric skirt.

Gabardine blazer.
Chiffon pleated skirt.

Cashmere
cloth jacket.
Crêpe skirt
with basque.

Double crêpe for
the jacket with
knotted collar.
Voile dégradé skirt.

Scalloped cashmere
sweater.
Wide tulle skirt.

Wool crêpe blouse.
Chiffon pleated skirt
with ruffled basque.

Taffeta cocktail
dress with
crêpe edges.

Double crêpe
scalloped suit.

Wool crêpe jacket.
Wide layered
tulle skirt.

Scalloped silk
crêpe blouse.
Dotted tulle skirt.

48 HOURS
IN
Miami Beach

48 HOURS IN MIAMI BEACH

TECHNIQUE:
ecoline.

MATERIALS:
thick watercolour
paper, ecoline,
grease pencils.

Draw the collection on white
A4 sheets or US letter. Using
an overhead projector transfer
the drawing onto watercolour
paper and clean up the drawing
with a kneaded eraser to
remove the excess graphite
and avoid spreading it over the
watercolour.

Finish the
drawing with
a 6B/8B
grease pencil.

Use Ecoline colours, which give
the effect of watercolours but
are completely transparent,
to create the desired colour.
Apply the highly diluted colour
first, wait for it to dry, and
then apply less diluted colour
to create chiaroscuro effects.

Muslin dress.
Honeycomb drape
and insert.

Cady jungle print mini dress.

Big flower
georgette dress.
Silk jersey
trousers.

Voile dress/blouse
on denim wash.

Silk satin
dress with
drawstring.

Honeycomb straps for
pleated muslin dress.

Satin dress
with ruffle
sleeves.

Torchon neckline
satin dress.

Silk chiffon blouse
with honeycomb
insert.

Gold satin
dress with
torchon straps.

Saturday light fever

TECHNIQUE: chalk on card. **MATERIALS:** dark smooth card, chalk pencils, smudge tool, 0.1/0.3/0.8 rapidograph, acrylic paint markers, coloured chalk.

Transfer the drawings onto the dark card using white copy paper.

If the drawing is not pronounced, go over it with a white crayon as required.

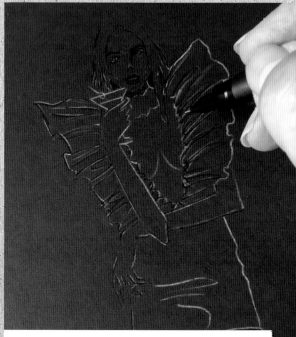

Go over the drawing with a rapidograph that is thicker on the outside and thinner on the inside.

Use a flesh-coloured chalk pencil to colour the face and other body parts. The chalk should be applied only at the points in light and is then blended in.

Use a smudge tool or a cotton swab to blend the chalk thus creating a chiaroscuro effect.

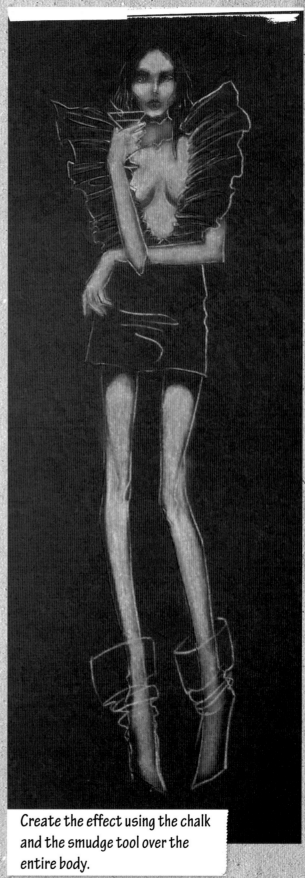

Create the effect using the chalk and the smudge tool over the entire body.

Also use chalk crayons colour and blend the various parts of the dress.

Use a black crayon to create shadow effects.

Obtain a sequin effect by making dots with acrylic markers of various shades, starting with the darkest and then moving through the lightest to white, but leaving darker areas in the folds and the parts in shade.

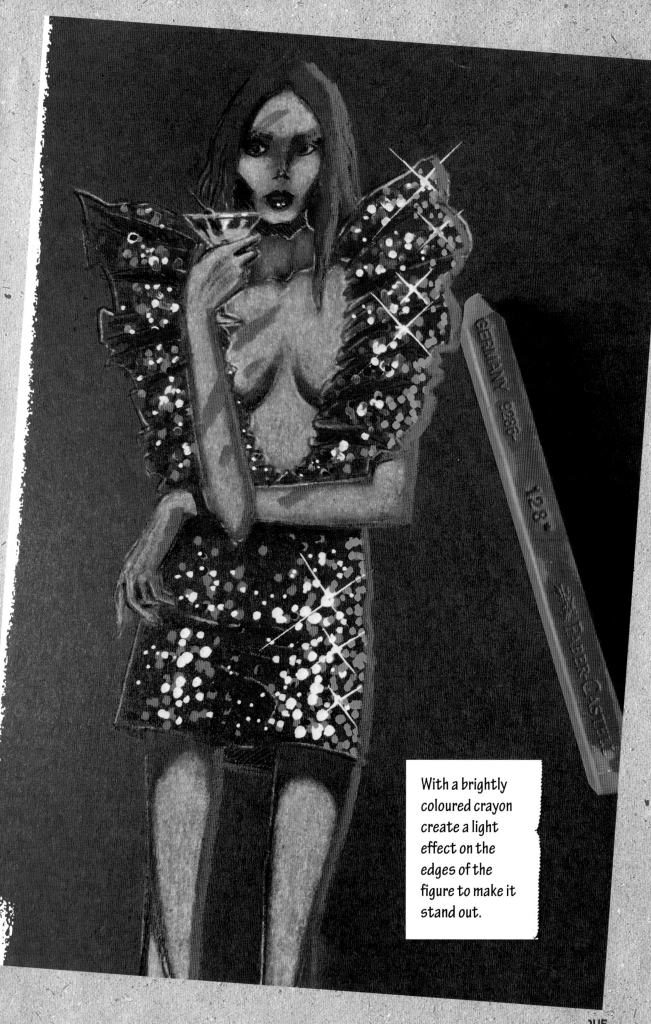

With a brightly coloured crayon create a light effect on the edges of the figure to make it stand out.

Sequin embroidered mini evening dress with wide ruffle neckline.

Mini full sequined
sheath dress
with wide leg of
mutton sleeves.

Asymmetrical latex sheath dress with wide sequin embroidered sleeves. Transparent PVC boots.

Sequined mini sheath dress with light multilayer tulle ruffle.

Dress with embroidered full sequined bodice and patent leather skirt.

Sequined mini
dress with deep V
neckline and latex
puff sleeves.

Gold sequined mini dress bustier with rigid patent leather drape.

Asymmetrical sequined mini dress with bustier and long sleeves.

Patent leather
sequined mini dress.

Pink latex mini dress with wide sleeves in sequin embroidered tulle.

URBAN COWBOY

TECHNIQUE: watercolour tempera.
MATERIAL: semi-rough ice grey card, tempera, grease and wax crayons, 9B grease pencil.

After transferring the design onto the card using an overhead projector or copy paper, use tempera to create the colour of the complexion and dilute it with plenty of water. Apply the colour with a No. 6 brush.

To create the colour of the complexion add a hint of red and yellow to the white to obtain a very soft colour.

Use blue mixed with black to create the colour of denim and dilute it with plenty of water. Apply a thin layer of this colour.

Add less water to get a more pronounced colour for the jacket and bag.

Once the basic colour is perfectly dry, use grease or wax crayons to create a pattern on the fabric.

Use a grease pencil to finish the drawing and create some shadow points with a black crayon.

Glazed cloth oversize jacket. Denim skirt with flounces.

Raw glazed cloth blazer. Denim and washed silk ruffled skirt.

Herringbone wool jacket with fringes. Men's jeans with grosgrain edging.

Herringbone blazer with wide cashmere lapel. Glazed tweed pants.

Polka dot
washed silk
day dress
with ruffles.
Bleached
leather bag.

Day dress
in checked
cotton muslin
with flounces.
Leather
saddlebag.

Plaid wool
poncho vest.
Bleached glazed
denim trousers.

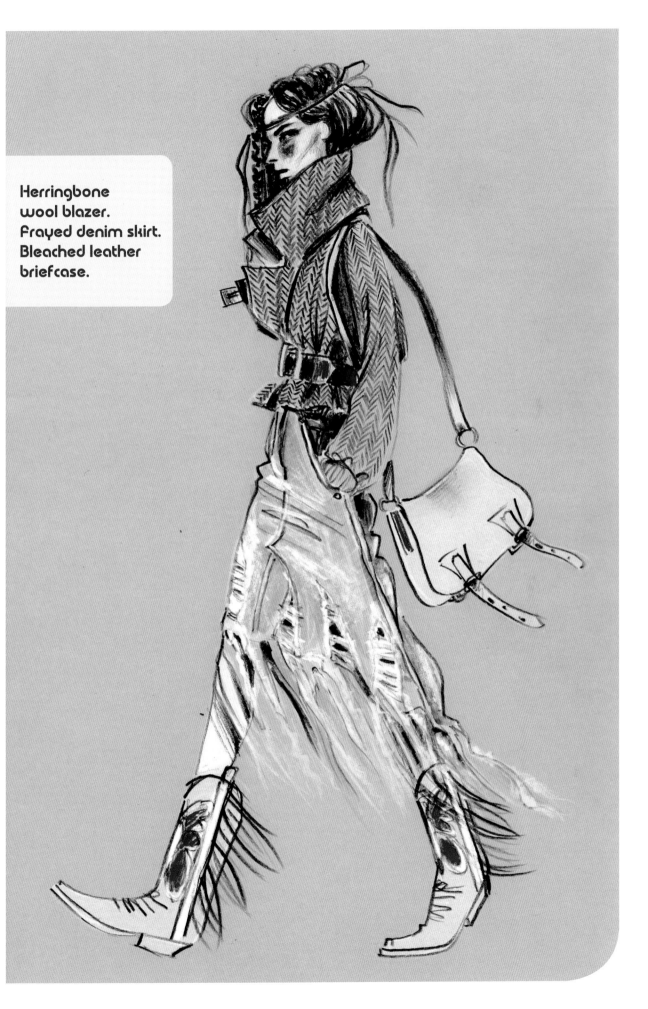

Herringbone
wool blazer.
Frayed denim skirt.
Bleached leather
briefcase.

Plain knit tartan wool cape jacket with fringed pockets. Printed reindeer trousers.

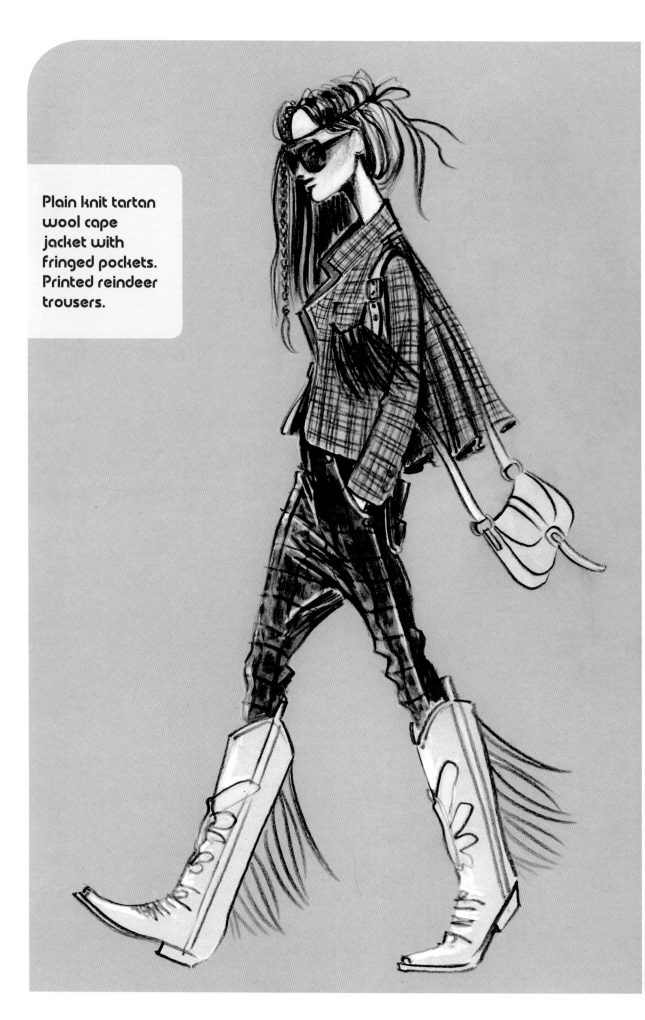

Oversize denim jacket with checkered flannel shirt. Herringbone tweed trousers.

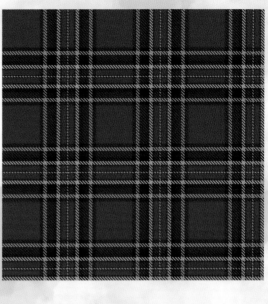

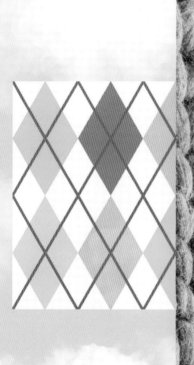

SCOTTISH
WOOL

TECHNIQUE: crayon and wax.
MATERIAL: blue smooth card, watercolour and grease wax crayons, 10B pencil.

Transfer the drawing onto the card using an overhead projector. Apply a light white layer to the face and uncovered parts of the body, then go over them with a slightly pinkish crayon.

Colour facial details such as eyebrows and lips with grease crayons to create make-up.

Define facial features with a grease pencil.

Use coloured crayons to give an initial colour base to the hair.

Create a second layer of hair colour using grease wax crayons of various shades of the same colour.

Use coloured crayons to define the texture of the dress keeping the colour of the card as the background.

With grease wax crayons, which give a denser effect, create the look of heavy knits and fur.

Leave some blank spaces between each pass of the wax crayon, so that parts of the card remain visible to give a chiaroscuro effect.

Tartan wool quilted jacket. Padded wool pinafore with visible edges. Houndstooth cloth trousers.

Plain wood coat with
Mongolian lapels.
Wool knit suit.

3/4 tartan cloth
quilted jacket.
Braided maxi
pullover dress.

Quilted coat in plaid wool
cloth and nylon polyester.
Suit with maxi knitted
pullover and ribbed leggings.

Patchwork effect
wool houndstooth
quilted cape jacket.
Plain knit tartan
jumpsuit.

Oversize 3/4 wool
cloth coat with
polyester nylon
quilted sleeves.
Knitted maxi
pullover dress.

Asymmetrical tartan wool quilted jacket. Cable knit leggings.

Plaid padded wool
coat with Mongolian
edging and ribbed
bomber sleeves.
Oversize knitted dress.

Diamond
pattern knit
maxi dress
with pockets.
Long coarse
wool scarf.

Tartan plain
knit wool cloth
quilted jacket.
Overalls with
knitted leggings.
Plaid scarf.

Tapisserie

TAPISSERIE

TECHNIQUE:
collage.
MATERIALS:
thick ribbed card,
texture paper,
tracing paper,
pantone, grease
pencil, transparent
adhesive paper.

Transfer the drawing onto the
card using white copy paper.

Print a full size face
taken from the web
or scanned from a
fashion magazine.
Cut out the face
and paste it.

Place the tracing paper over the drawing and draw various models of the parts of the dress. Fix them onto the texture paper with pins and cut out the different parts. You can find these papers printed in various fashion magazines or you can print them from the internet.

Glue the different parts onto the card to construct the model, then with a dark grey pantone create a chiaroscuro directly on the texture paper.

Use a grease pencil to define the parts of the model like folds and seams.

Outline the shadows of the trousers with the grey pantone, using the card itself for the texture. Finally, finish the trousers using a grease pencil again.

Cut out a shape in the form of a pair of glasses out of the transparent adhesive paper and apply it to the figure.

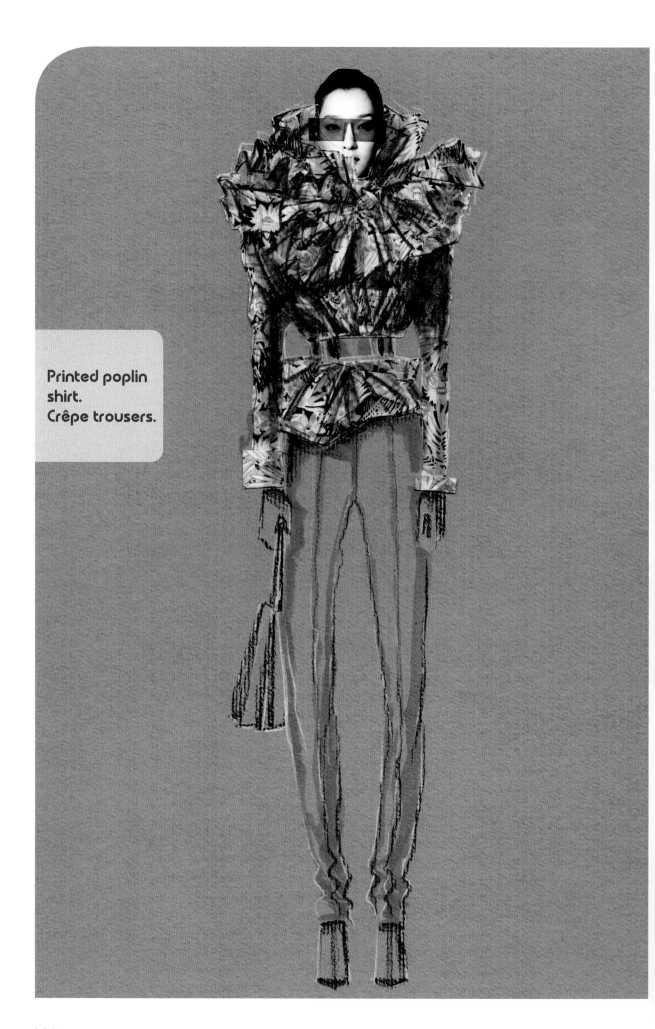

Printed poplin
shirt.
Crêpe trousers.

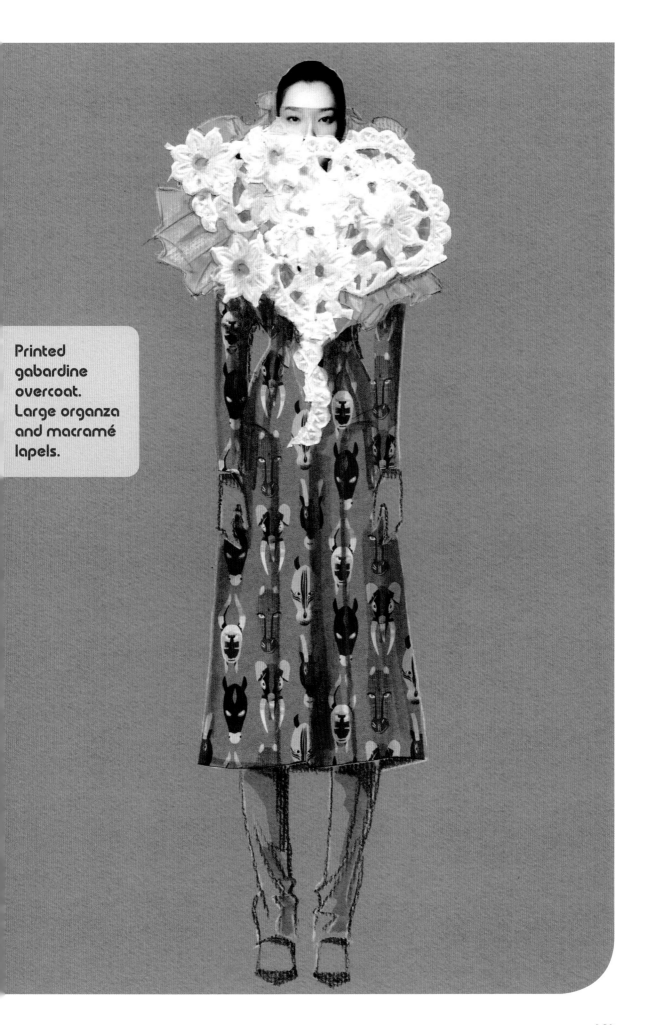

Printed
gabardine
overcoat.
Large organza
and macramé
lapels.

Raw linen jacket
suit with ruffle.
Crêpe trousers.
Tulle skirt.

Tulle blouse
with wide silk
satin collar.
Linen pants.

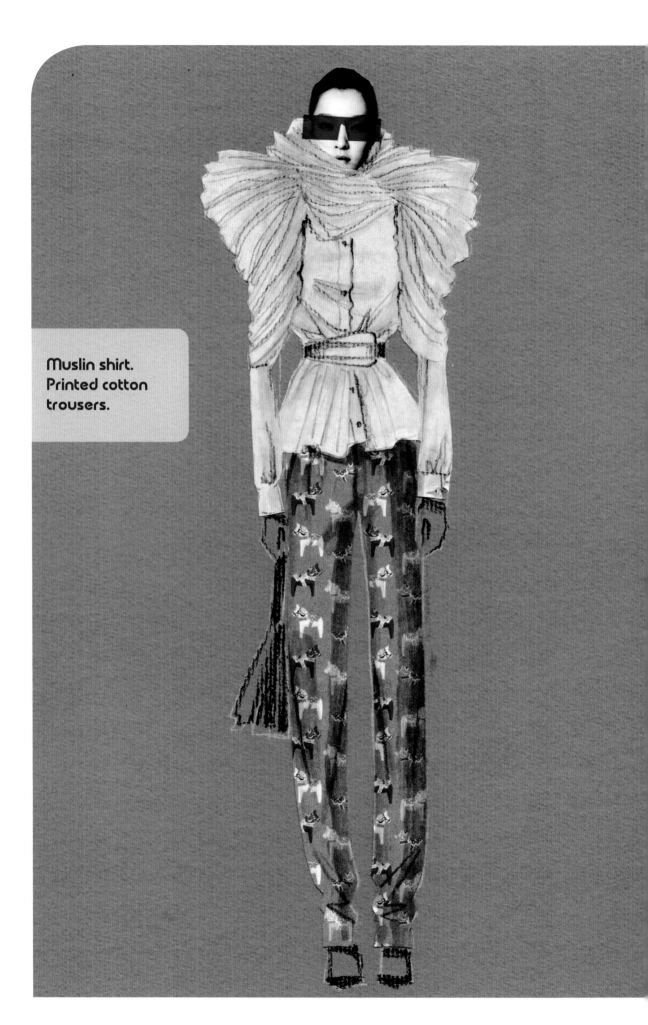

Muslin shirt.
Printed cotton
trousers.

Chiffon
chemisier.
Silk ribbon
collar.
Cady trousers.

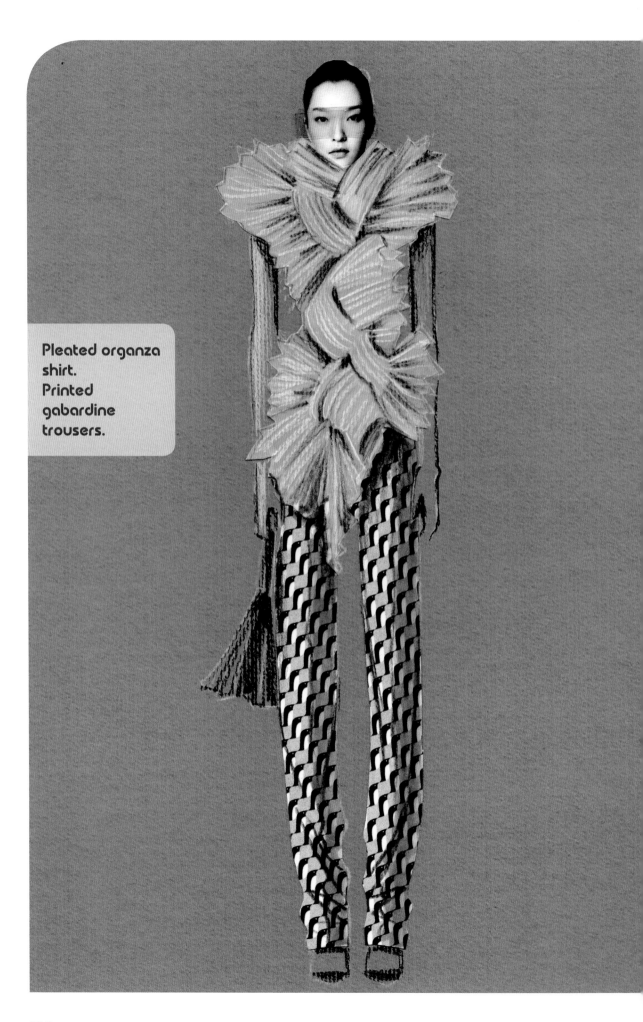

Pleated organza shirt. Printed gabardine trousers.

Printed cotton
canvas screwed
blazer with
poplin collar like
the skirt
with gauze
petticoat.

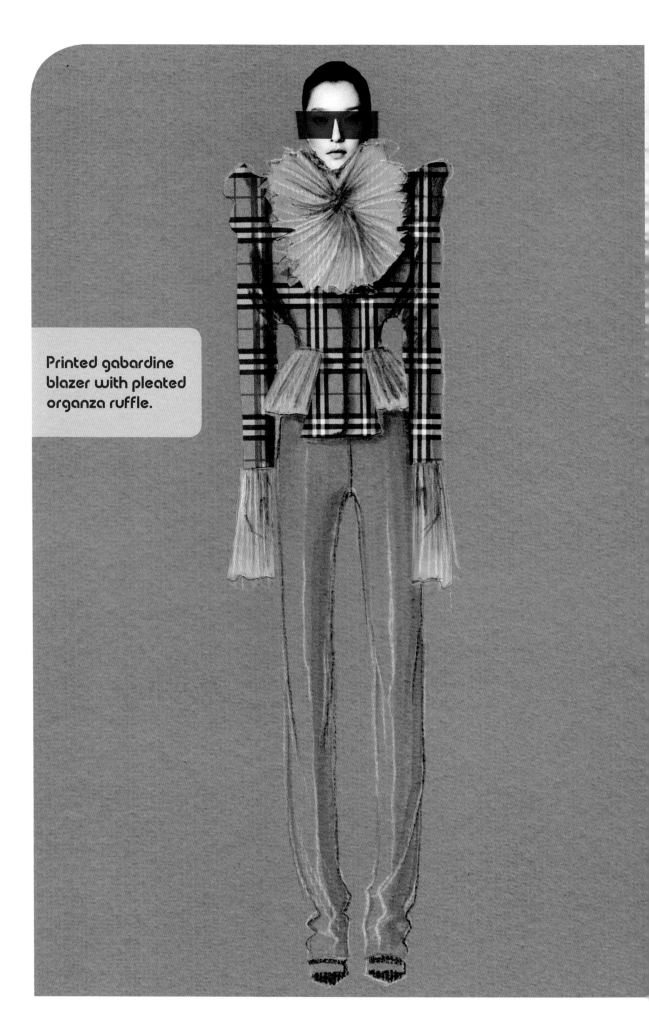

Printed gabardine blazer with pleated organza ruffle.

Blazer with
structured lapels.
Pleated organza
skirt.
Cady trousers.

TECHNIQUE:
dry tempera.
MATERIALS:
rigid grey mixed
media card,
tempera, wax
crayons, grease
pencil.

Transfer the drawing
onto the card
using copy paper.

Flat brushes of
various sizes
are used for this
technique.

Go over the drawing with a grease pencil so that it is clearly visible.

Create the colour and brush on dry with small strokes, pressing the flat brush open to create the effect of hair.

When the base colour is dry go over it with a darker shade to give a chiaroscuro effect. Also using dry tempera and a smaller brush you can make more designs and decorations.

Continue until the hair looks realistic.

As you can see, no water has been added to the tempera. Make sure you dry the brush well after washing it, before dipping it in the next colour.

Use the wax crayons to finish the rest of the model.

Also using a flat brush and dry tempera create light spots. Make sure you wait for the colour to dry well before the next step.

Create a large knit effect with grease wax crayons.

With light touches of wax crayon you can create transparent effects.

After applying the colour using wax and tempera, finish each part of the drawing with a grease pencil.

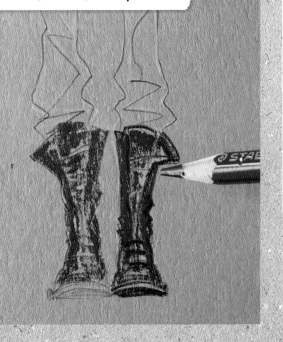

Finally, finish the face with a very sharp grease pencil, using the colour of the cardboard as the base.

Long pile faux fur blazer with cartoon print.

Cavallino leather and printed fur manteau coat.

Faux fur with cartoon print. Muslin dress.

Degradé printed
faux fur.
Crêpe chemisier.

Faux fur hood
with street
art print.
Voile chemisier.

Cavallino leather and brocade coat with faux fur cartoon print lapels.

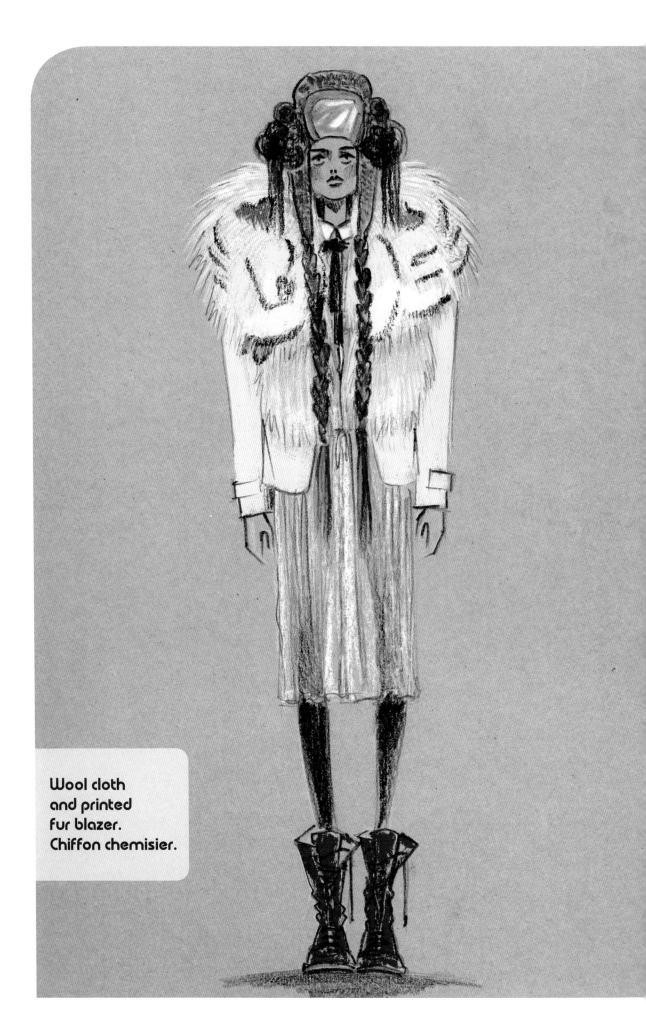

Wool cloth
and printed
fur blazer.
Chiffon chemisier.

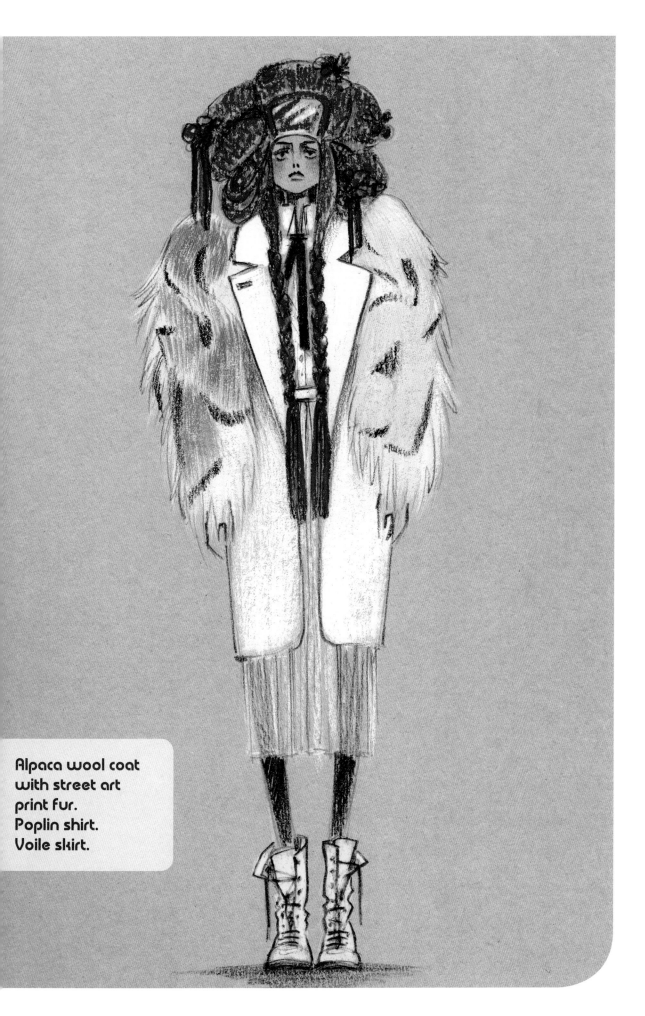

Alpaca wool coat
with street art
print fur.
Poplin shirt.
Voile skirt.

Wool crêpe tunic dress with printed fur sleeves and pockets.

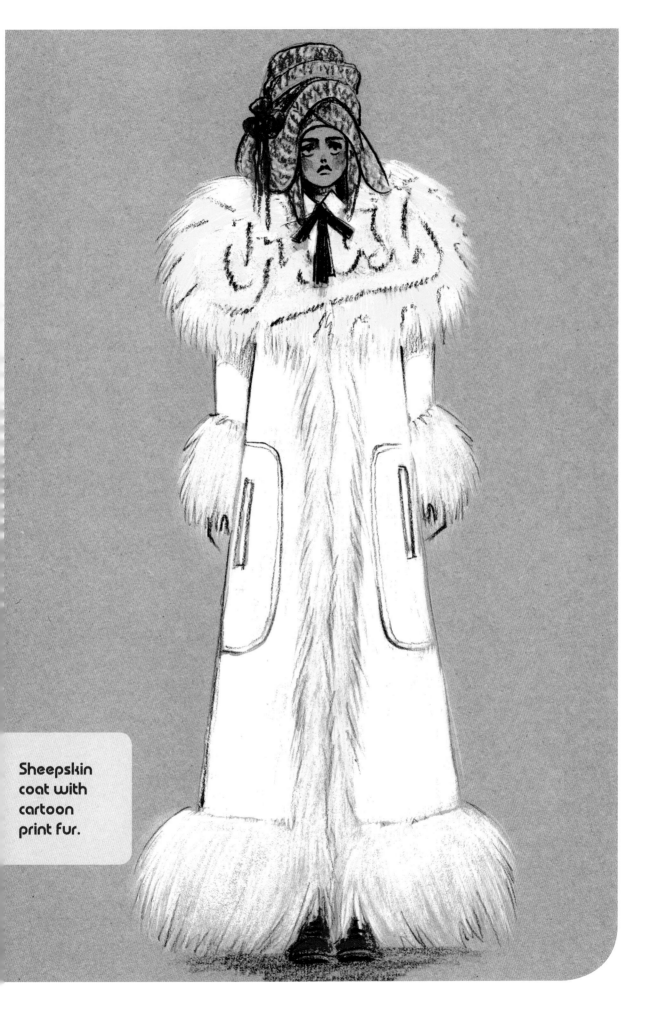

Sheepskin coat with cartoon print fur.

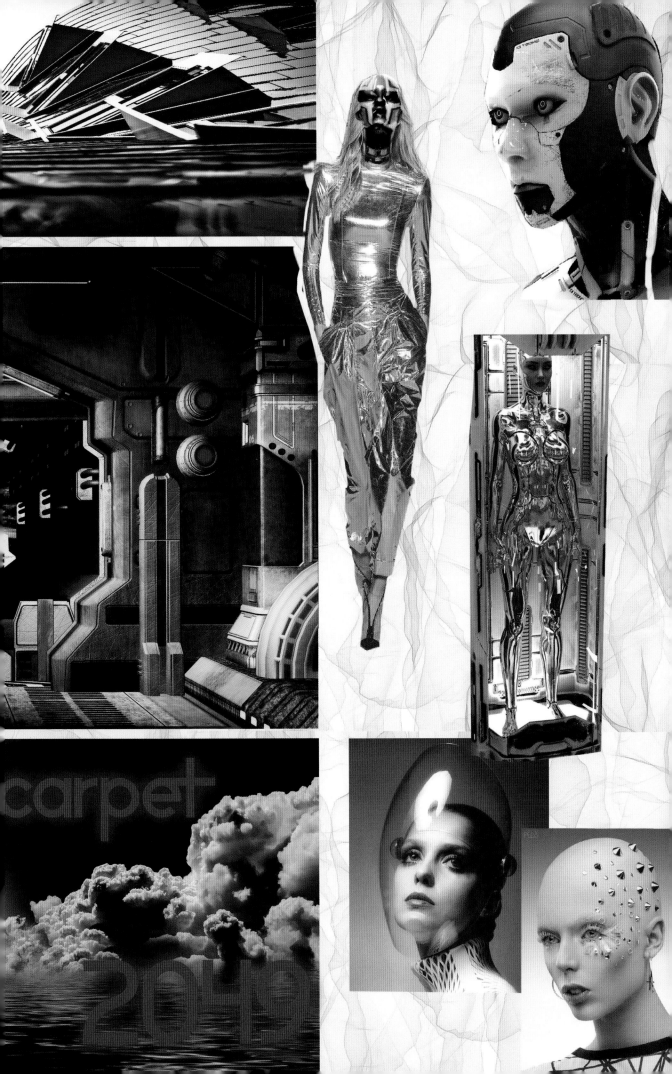

RED CARPET 2049

TECHNIQUE: digital photocomposition. **MATERIAL:** ipad, Procreate app.

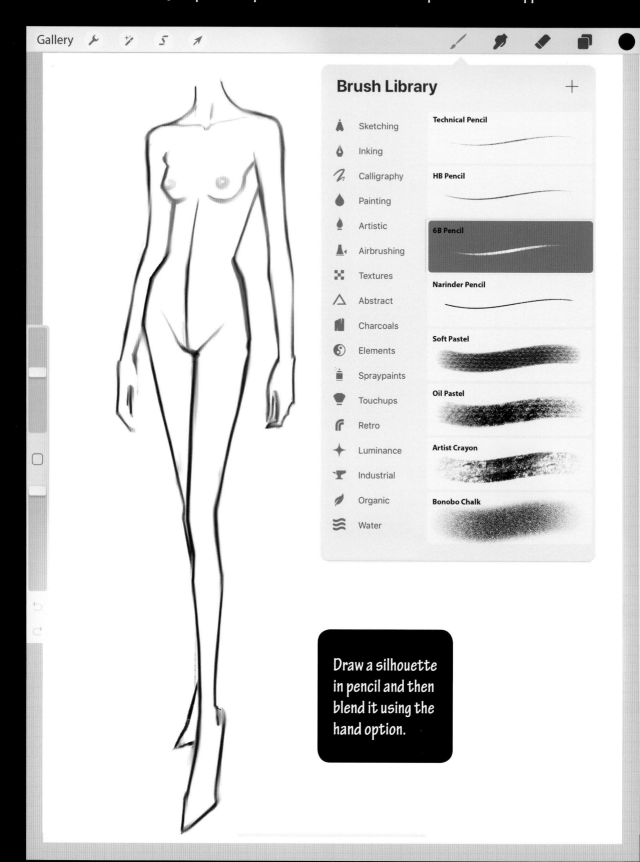

Draw a silhouette in pencil and then blend it using the hand option.

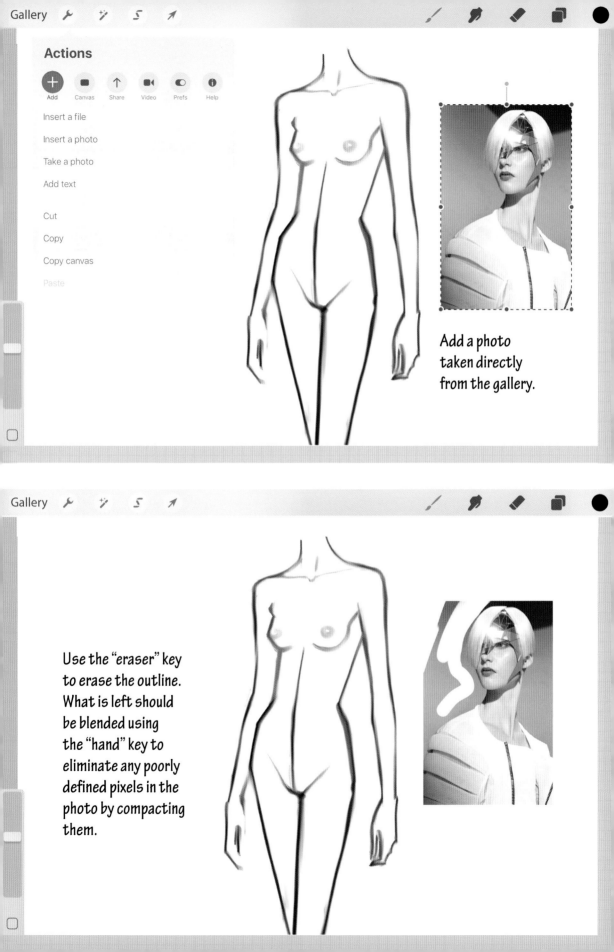

Actions

Insert a file

Insert a photo

Take a photo

Add text

Cut

Copy

Copy canvas

Paste

Add a photo taken directly from the gallery.

Use the "eraser" key to erase the outline. What is left should be blended using the "hand" key to eliminate any poorly defined pixels in the photo by compacting them.

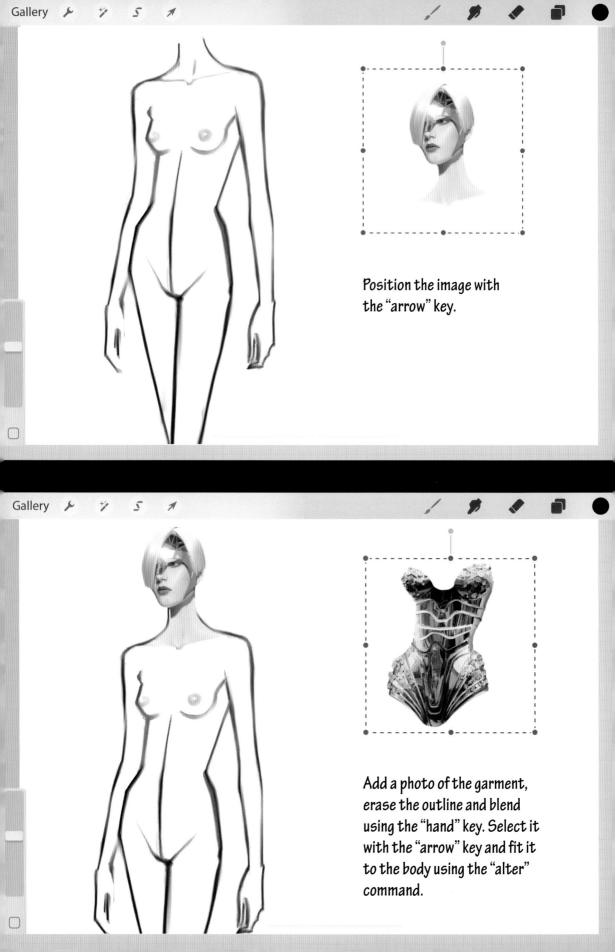

Position the image with the "arrow" key.

Add a photo of the garment, erase the outline and blend using the "hand" key. Select it with the "arrow" key and fit it to the body using the "alter" command.

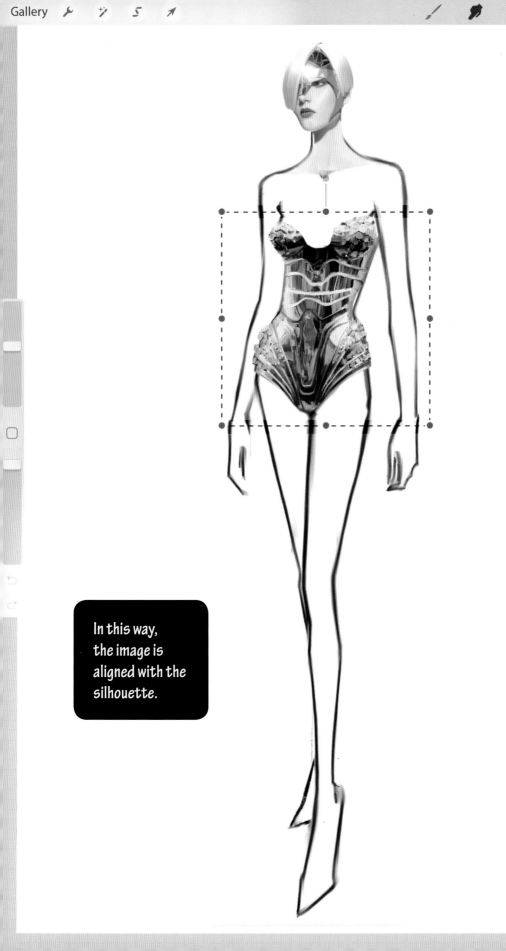

In this way,
the image is
aligned with the
silhouette.

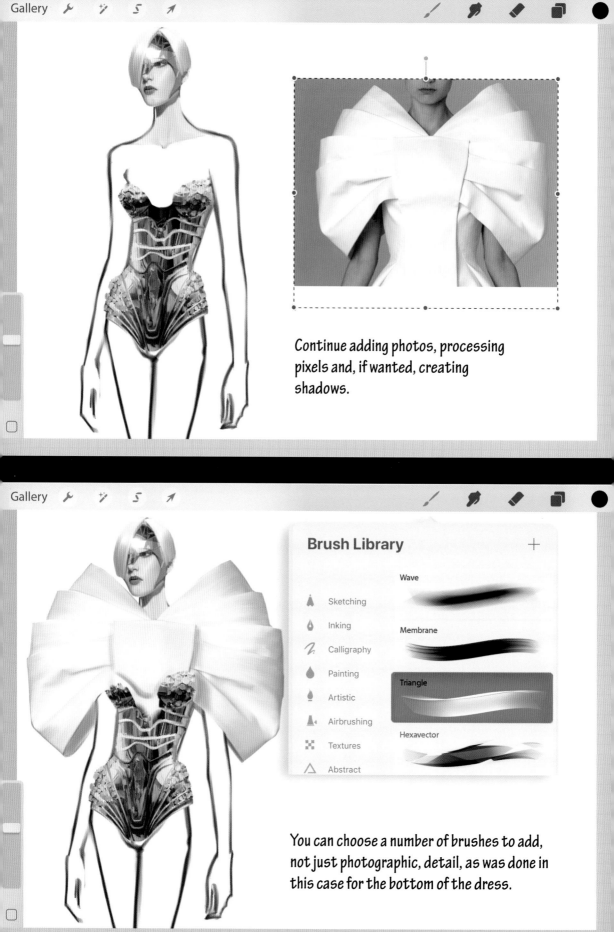

Continue adding photos, processing
pixels and, if wanted, creating
shadows.

Brush Library

Wave

Sketching

Inking

Membrane

Calligraphy

Painting

Triangle

Artistic

Airbrushing

Hexavector

Textures

Abstract

You can choose a number of brushes to add,
not just photographic, detail, as was done in
this case for the bottom of the dress.

Abstract and marbled brush.

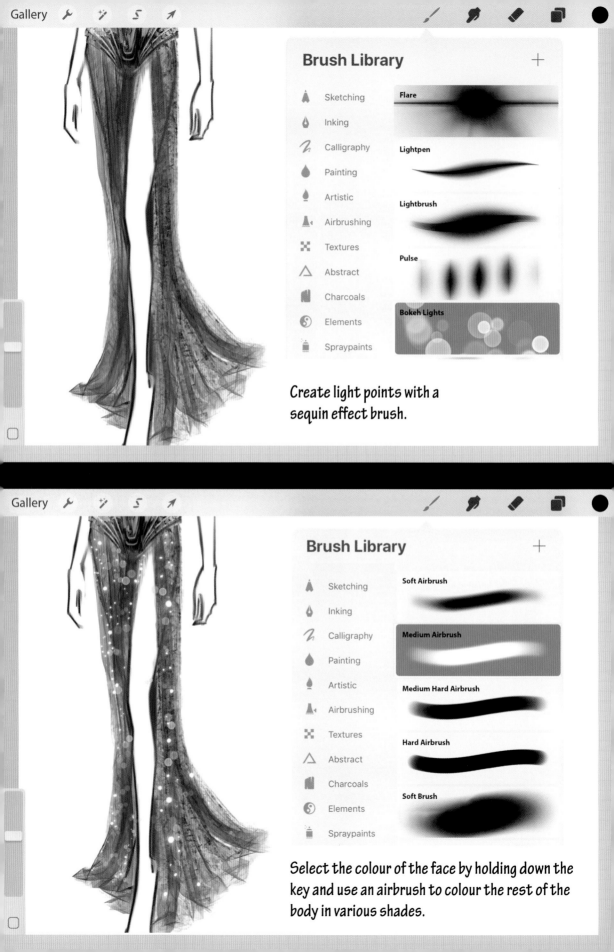

Brush Library

Sketching
Inking
Calligraphy
Painting
Artistic
Airbrushing
Textures
Abstract
Charcoals
Elements
Spraypaints

Flare

Lightpen

Lightbrush

Pulse

Bokeh Lights

Create light points with a sequin effect brush.

Brush Library

Sketching
Inking
Calligraphy
Painting
Artistic
Airbrushing
Textures
Abstract
Charcoals
Elements
Spraypaints

Soft Airbrush

Medium Airbrush

Medium Hard Airbrush

Hard Airbrush

Soft Brush

Select the colour of the face by holding down the key and use an airbrush to colour the rest of the body in various shades.

Layers

	Inserted image	N	☑
	Inserted image	N	☑
	Inserted image	N	☑
	Inserted image	N	☑
	Inserted image	N	☑
	Inserted image	N	☑
	Inserted image	N	☑
	Background colour		☑

Make sure you create a new layer for each part. By adding photographs, however, the layer creates itself.

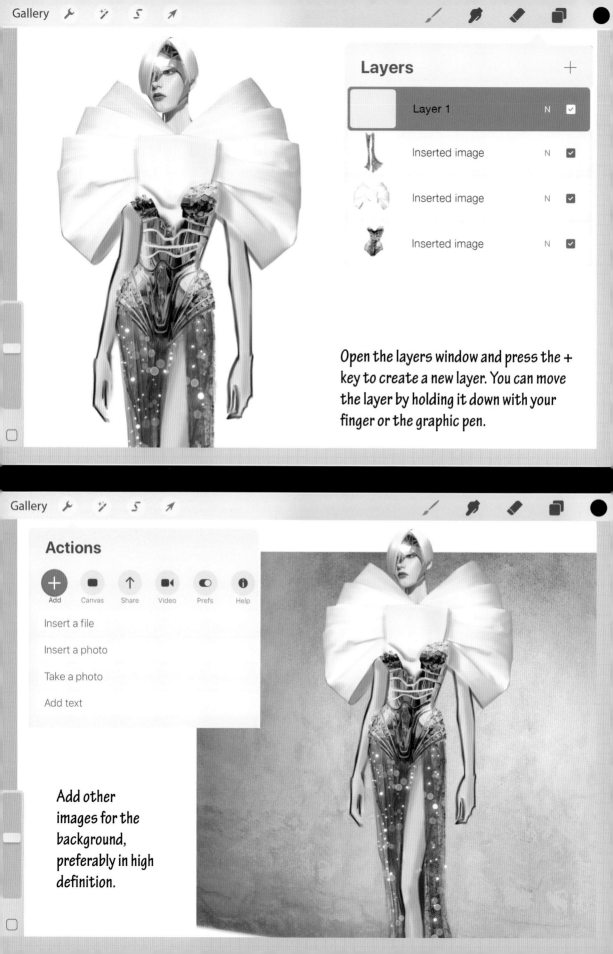

Layers

Layer 1   N

Inserted image   N

Inserted image   N

Inserted image   N

Open the layers window and press the + key to create a new layer. You can move the layer by holding it down with your finger or the graphic pen.

Actions

Add   Canvas   Share   Video   Prefs   Help

Insert a file

Insert a photo

Take a photo

Add text

Add other images for the background, preferably in high definition.

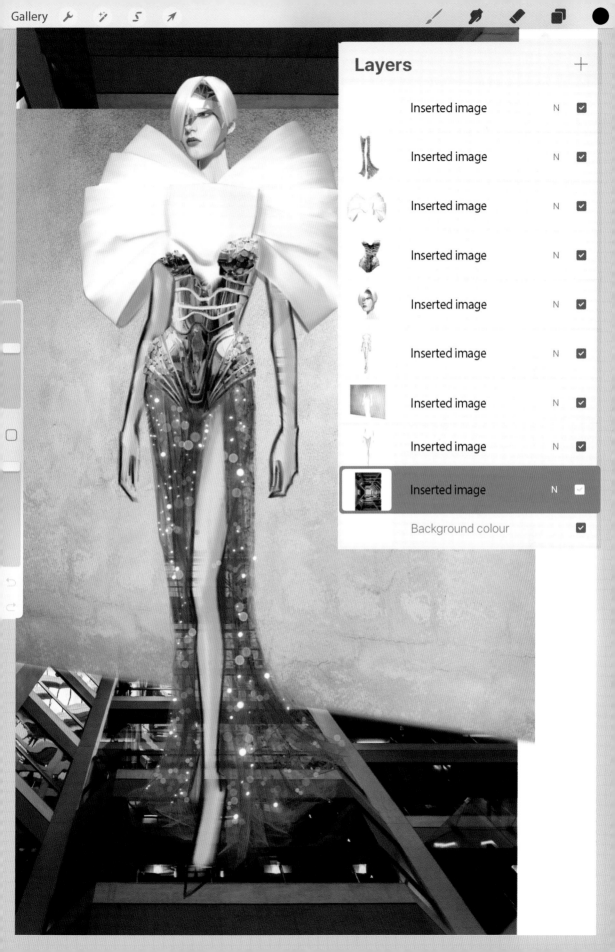

Layers

Inserted image   N   ☑

Inserted image   N   ☑

Inserted image   N   ☑

Inserted image   N   ☑

Inserted image   N   ☑

Inserted image   N   ☑

Inserted image   N   ☑

Inserted image   N   ☑

Inserted image   N   ☑

Background colour   ☑

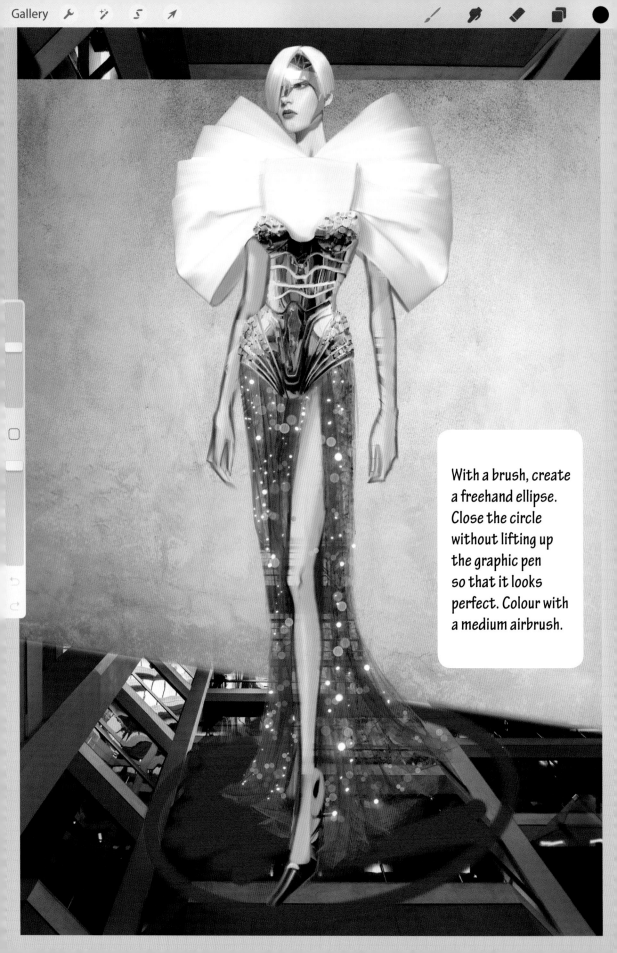

With a brush, create a freehand ellipse. Close the circle without lifting up the graphic pen so that it looks perfect. Colour with a medium airbrush.

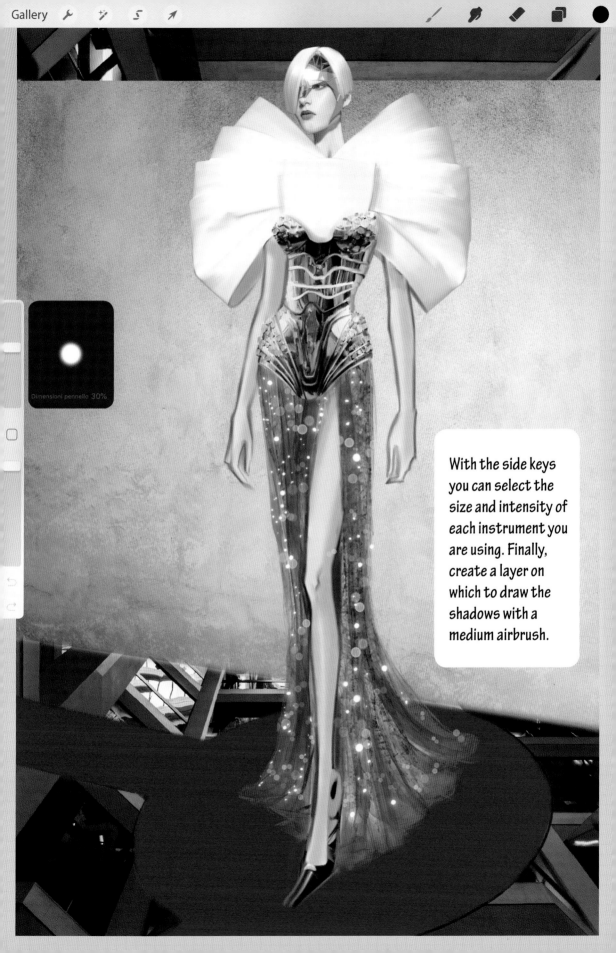

Dimensioni pennello 30%

With the side keys
you can select the
size and intensity of
each instrument you
are using. Finally,
create a layer on
which to draw the
shadows with a
medium airbrush.

Grand soirée dress.
Flexible metal
bustier with poplin
cape shirt neckline.
Doubled and
embroidered
chiffon skirt
with maxi
transparent sequins.

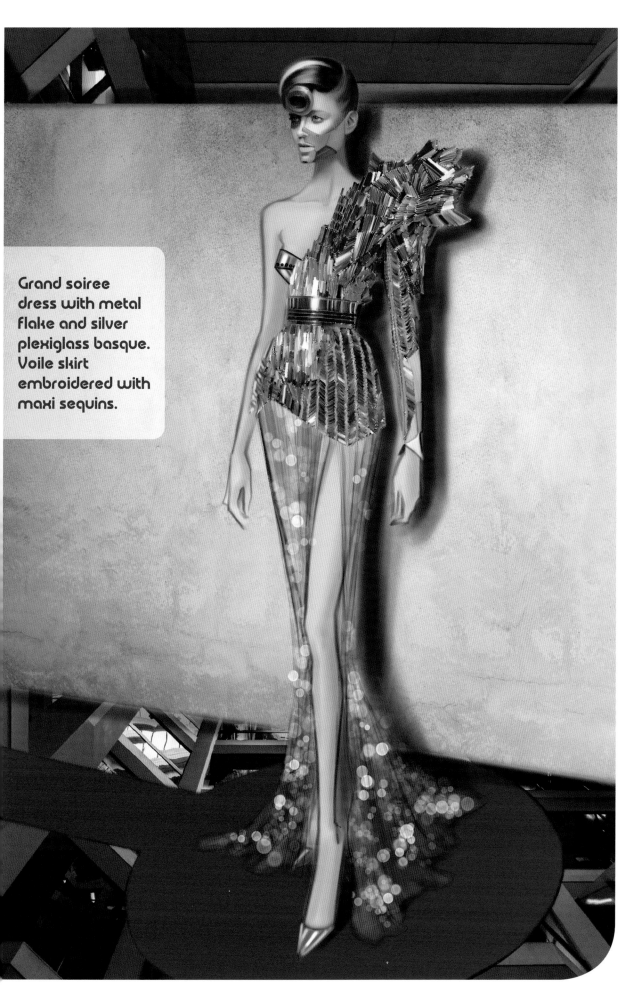

Grand soiree dress with metal flake and silver plexiglass basque. Voile skirt embroidered with maxi sequins.

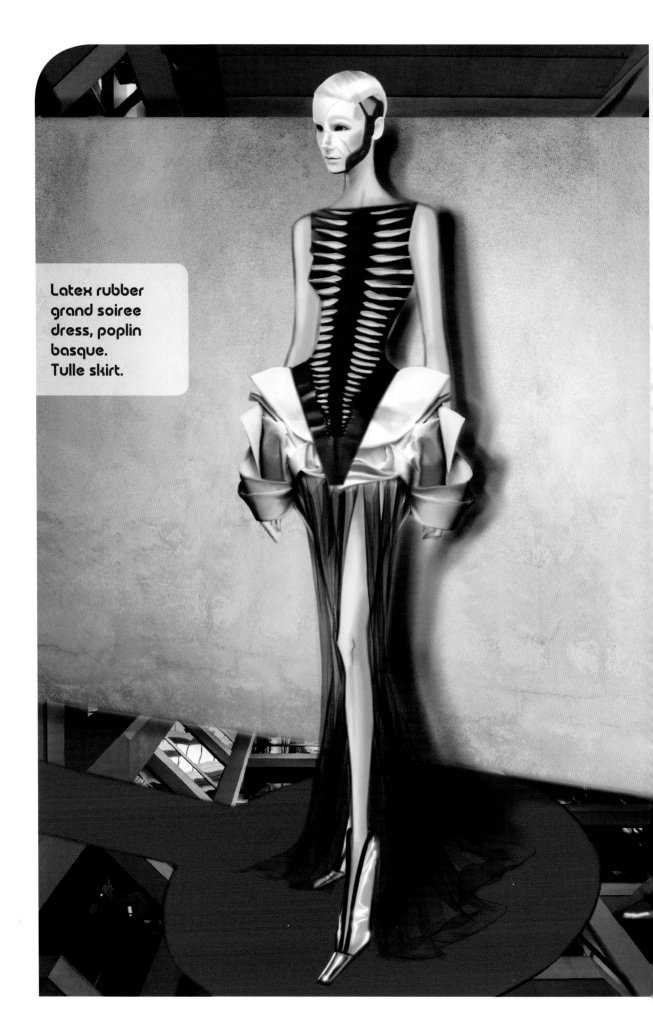

Latex rubber grand soiree dress, poplin basque. Tulle skirt.

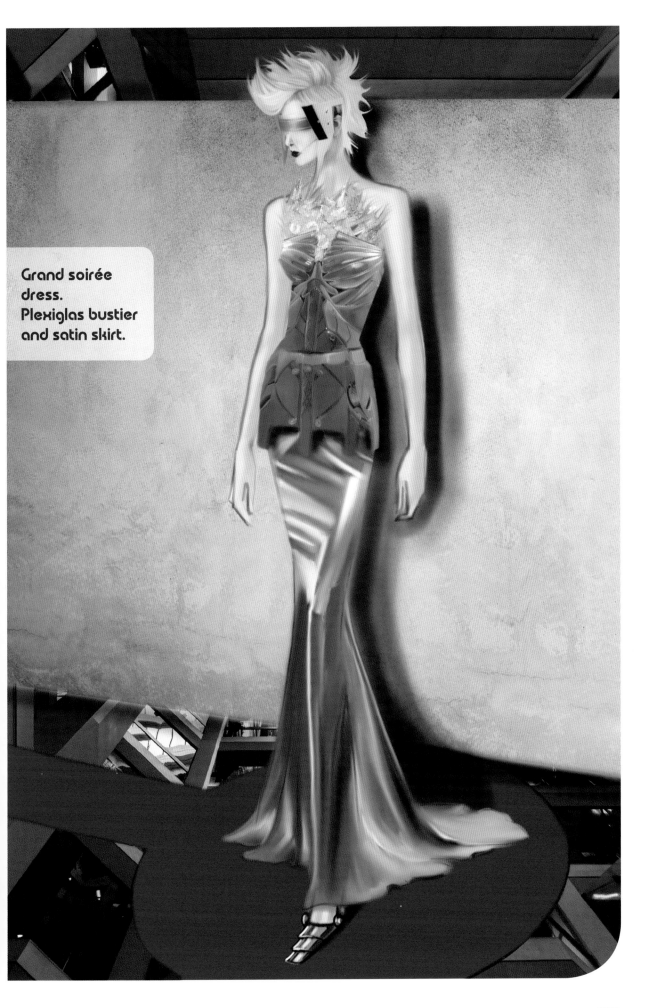

Grand soirée
dress.
Plexiglas bustier
and satin skirt.

Grand soirée dress.
Poplin shrug.
Embroidered
studded neoprene
bustier. Chiffon
skirt with dégradé
embroidery.

Faux leather grand
soirée dress.
Wide amphora skirt.
Flexible metal
turtleneck bustier.

Rubberised leather grand soiree dress. Dégradé embroidered tulle skirt.

Grand soirée dress with neoprene basque. Tulle skirt.

Grand soirée dress with metal plates. Stitched neoprene shrug.

Grand soirée dress with Plexiglas and silicone bustier. Cracked flaked patent leather sleeves and satin dévoré skirt.

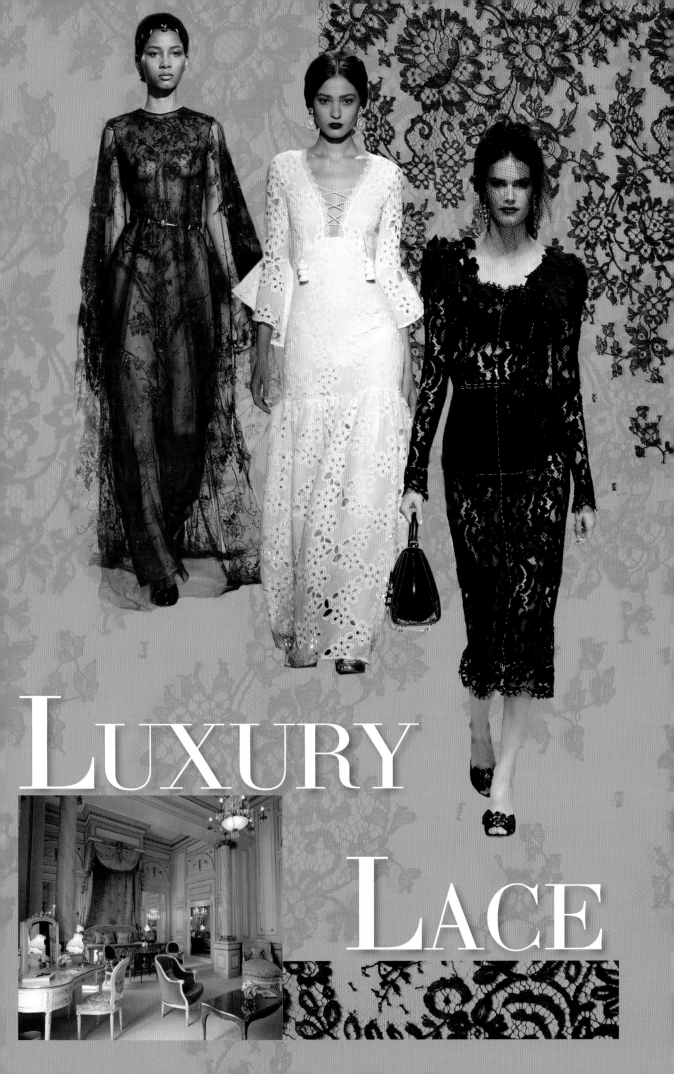

Luxury

Lace

LUXURY LACE

TECHNIQUE: digital with manual strokes. *MATERIAL:* ipad, Procreate app.

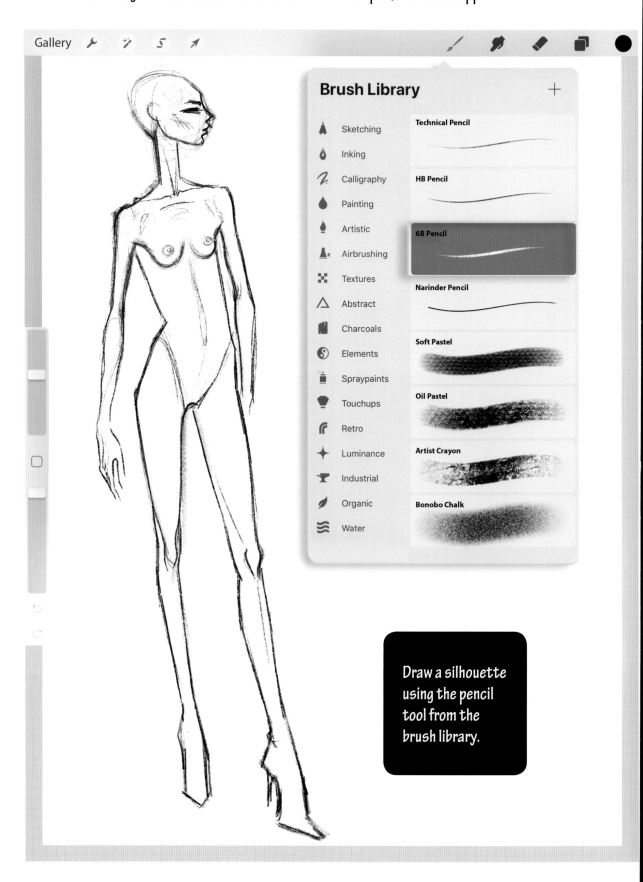

Draw a silhouette using the pencil tool from the brush library.

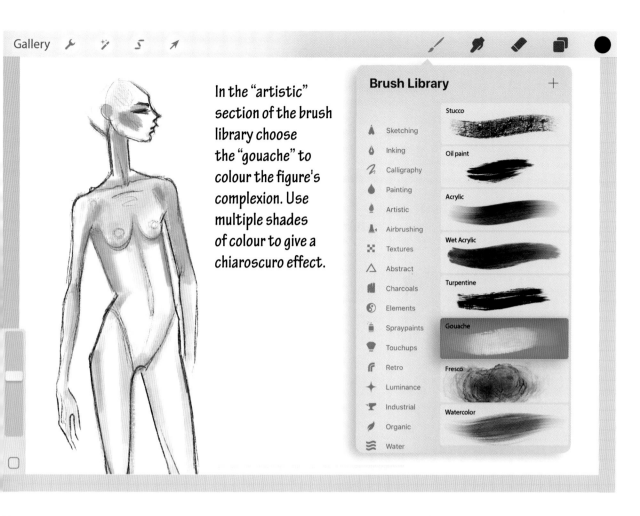

In the "artistic" section of the brush library choose the "gouache" to colour the figure's complexion. Use multiple shades of colour to give a chiaroscuro effect.

Brush Library +

Sketching
Inking
Calligraphy
Painting
Artistic
Airbrushing
Textures
Abstract
Charcoals
Elements
Spraypaints
Touchups
Retro
Luminance
Industrial
Organic
Water

Stucco
Oil paint
Acrylic
Wet Acrylic
Turpentine
Gouache
Fresco
Watercolor

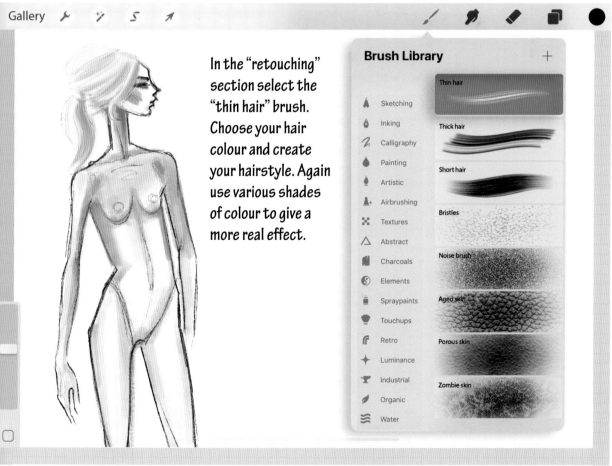

In the "retouching" section select the "thin hair" brush. Choose your hair colour and create your hairstyle. Again use various shades of colour to give a more real effect.

Brush Library +

Sketching
Inking
Calligraphy
Painting
Artistic
Airbrushing
Textures
Abstract
Charcoals
Elements
Spraypaints
Touchups
Retro
Luminance
Industrial
Organic
Water

Thin hair
Thick hair
Short hair
Bristles
Noise brush
Aged skin
Porous skin
Zombie skin

After adding a coloured background, draw the model with the pencil tool.

You can create brushes of any fabric by clicking on the + of the brush library and inserting a photo, then adjusting the intensity and pressure. Here the brush created with San Gallo lace was used. Brush it over the desired area.

Use the medium airbrush tool to create shadows on another level, with support from the "multiply" option. In this way the colour of the shadows will not hide the underlying lace design.

Use the airbrush tool to colour the bodice and its shadows on another level, adjusting the size of the brush.

To create the background the "faded Indian ink" brush from the "ink" section was used.

To create a more precise background you can use a photographic medium that will then be deleted.

Dress with straps and embroidered bustier, San Gallo lace skirt.

Macramé lace
dress.

Macramé shirt and skirt outfit.

Silk velvet and rebrodé lace dress.

Chantilly lace
house dress.

Tulle and
rebrodé lace
house dress.

San Gallo lace
ruffled dress.

Chantilly lace dress with satin inserts.

Silk velvet dress, lace skirt.

Chantilly lace dress.

PROMOPRESS FASHION COLLECTION

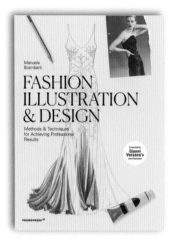

FASHION ILLUSTRATION & DESIGN
Methods & Techniques for Achieving Professional Results
Manuela Brambatti

978-84-16851-06-5
215 x 300 mm. 240 pp.

COLOUR IN FASHION ILLUSTRATION
Drawing and Painting Techniques
Tiziana Paci

978-84-16851-59-1
215 x 287 mm. 320 pp.

FASHION ILLUSTRATION & DESIGN ACCESSORIES
Shoes, Bags, Hats, Belts, Gloves and Glasses
Manuela Brambatti and Fabio Menconi

978-84-17412-64-7
210 x 297 mm. 264 pp.

FASHION DETAILS 4,000 DRAWINGS
Elisabetta Kuky Drudi

978-84-17412-68-5
195 x 285 mm. 384 pp.

Second Edition in 2020

PALETTE PERFECT
Color Combinations Inspired by Fashion, Art & Style
Lauren Wager

978-84-15967-90-3
148 x 210 mm. 304 pp.

FABRICS IN FASHION DESIGN
The Way Successful Fashion Designers Use Fabrics
Stefanella Sposito.
Photos by Gianni Pucci

978-84-16851-28-7
225 x 235 mm. 336 pp.